Natural Parenting

A Guide to Pregnancy, Birth, & Beyond

Published January 2007, Fort Collins, CO, USA
Copyright 2007 Hauslendale Publishing
ISBN # 978-0-6151-4905-9

Table of Contents

About the Author 9

Introduction 11

Exercise 1 15

First Moments

Exercise 2 31

Options

Exercise 3 63

Parental Vision

Exercise 4 73

The Soul Within

Exercise 5   85

Positive Visualization

Exercise 6   97

Birth & Beyond

Exercise 7   119

Breastfeeding

Exercise 8   155

Balance

Exercise 9   171

Lifestyle Parenting

Exercise 10   179

Nurturing Personalities

Some of us write letters to our friends to offer love, strength, and encouragement, and some of us write books.

About the Author

Author Meilena Hauslendale began her career at a very young age working as a journalist, freelance and contributing author. In 1997, Meilena embarked on her career as an inspirational artist, initially developing her style by displaying her art along with inspirational sayings. Her work was then featured internationally through galleries and publications. It wasn't until 2002, that she began publishing her writing in the form of personal development articles and books.

She is the author of *Making Your Purpose Your Business, Recognizing Unhealthy Relationships, The Spiritual Revolution*, and now *Natural Parenting: Guide to Pregnancy, Birth, & Beyond*.

The unique combination of art and literature had drawn recognition from both the art and writing community. In 2004, she was inducted into **Who's Who of American Women for 2004-2005,** the definitive biographical resource featuring the most accomplished women in all areas of human endeavor.

Meilena continues to write and exhibit her art, but always is a full-time mother to her two sons who have inspired this book.

To read more about Meilena, please visit us at:

http://www.inspirationalauthor.com

and

http://www.meilena.com

Introduction

I actually began writing this book during my second pregnancy in what I believe to be the 6th or 7th month. I began thinking of the concept of a natural parenting book at the onset of finding out I was pregnant again, but didn't think I would actually embark on the concept until after the birth of our child. However, as I began this journey once again, I was soon reminded of how our society views birth and the difference between how nature and spirituality view birth.

Birth alone is often characterized as a medical condition rather than a natural process of our world evolving. When left alone to nature's own devices, the process itself can be complete and successful with little or no intervention.

Birth alone is not the only natural concept we will face as we enter parenthood. Our responsibility to nature and the spiritual world does not stop at birth alone. In fact, it continues on into parenthood and childhood, where we as human beings will be constantly presented with choices between unnatural and natural. We are faced with the idea of whether we want a society to raise our children or whether we want to raise our children.

Somewhere along the way we have taken the emphasis off of what truly matters to us in our livelihoods. We have gotten busy with the mundane fundamentals of life and somehow negated our responsibilities to ourselves and our families. Instead of performing research and realizing our options in birth and in parenting, we wait for someone to 'tell' us the rights and wrongs. Perhaps thinking there is someone else in higher authority than ourselves and our own spiritual guidance.

In some instances, the uninformed parent can be taken advantage of and convinced that there is only one way to birth and raise a child. That there is only one stream of protocol which we are to follow and this book is here to tell you that this is not true. There is more out there. There are options, but you have to be willing to investigate them on your own and then make an educated decision based on your research.

Becoming a parent is not always a choice, but consider it a privilege. Your gift to this world is the fruit you bare to it. Birthing and raising a child in this world allows you many opportunities for growth as a person. It allows you to correct your own behaviors or some how see them through a different light. It allows you make corrections of that which may have ailed your own childhood. Now you have the opportunity to make a difference in yourself, your life, and your offering to the world.

There will be several exercises after the end of each chapter that will help you evaluate and determine your own structure and opinions. Part of learning about your own opinions and behaviors is also learning about where your primary influences stem from. From there you can dissect your influences and determine whether they are suitable for the life you want to live now as a parent. Your goal during this process is to become patient with yourself, just as you would be patient with a child learning for the very first time in their life.

This book will allow you the opportunity to become aware of the natural forms of birth and beyond. Our concept here is to not only learn how to make responsible choices, but also more natural choices, by looking at some of the influences that society, or family have convinced are correct. We are appointed to find the truth that is right for us and we do this by removing the fear to ask questions.

Although we may cover several chapters or discuss choices that focus on a women's right, please note this does not exclude a man from becoming informed about birth and parenting. Even alternative life partners are not excluded from this role of influence. If you are going to raise a child whether alone or with a partner, regardless of your gender, you have a responsibility that needs to be nurtured and informed. Take action, assess your role, and contribute a responsible influence as the actions you take now affect the world as a whole.

Exercise 1

the FIRST MOMENTS

The very first moment you find out you are going to become a parent, there can be so much emotion that occurs inside. You can be excited and you can be fearful all at the same time. Just the mere fact that you are going to be responsible for bringing another human being into this world can be rather intimidating.

All of a sudden your lifestyle becomes impacted. Your living arrangements and your behaviors take a new precedence in your life. What may have been permissible for you and your partner may take a turn into a new adventure into the unknown world of parenting.

Any irresponsible behavior becomes amplified because now not only does it affect you as a person, but also the child you are getting ready to raise.

The innocence of a child makes us look more clearly at who we are, and the impact that we have on their ability to learn, and articulate our behaviors. Before a child develops their own behavior and stature, they learn by mimicking and replicating the behaviors they see around them.

In truth, we are faced with the reality of ourselves. Even though the child is inside the womb, our shift of responsibilities, thoughts and inhibitions, take on a more active role in our conscious thoughts than before.

Everyone reacts differently when they find out for the first time that they are going to be a parent. The reality, for some, can be that they do not want to be a part of this process. Perhaps the relationship that created this child was not out of love, but convenience. In this situation, the woman is faced with the choice and decision of whether or not to raise the child on her own and carry on with her pregnancy.

If the woman chooses adoption or abortion then her choice for being a parent at that particular time in her life was passed on. If she chose to accept the challenge of parenthood, regardless of whether a partner was in her life or not, then she is embarking on a journey she will never forget.

Men and women play very different roles when it comes to preparing for the birth of a child. There honestly is no paper cut-out of how one will act or react, when they find out they are going to be a parent. For men, reality may not sink in until they see their partner's belly growing. Women however, are forced to face the reality very early on, because the changes that are occurring to them are not just emotional, but also physical.

If the woman's partner is in-tune to what they are feeling, they will actually experience similar pregnancy symptoms and emotions. Men can experience cravings for certain food, morning sickness, weight gain and mood fluctuations. All of which subside when the pregnancy is complete and the child is born. This is called the Couvade Syndrome or *Sympathetic Pregnancy*.

Some men are not connected with the mother nor do they want to be connected with the child. They may be in denial and bypass discussions on becoming a father. They may avoid the pregnancy and no longer carry on a relationship with the mother. They may literally run away from the pregnancy and relocate so that they do not have to face it at all.

When it comes to pregnancy both men and women have the option of fight or flight. How a person chooses to react to pregnancy reflects how they choose to react to themselves. The questions we have to ask ourselves are:

a. Have we dealt with ourselves yet?

b. Do we know what type of life we want to lead in front of our child?

c. What fears do you have about becoming a parent?

d. What changes would you want to make before the child was born?

e. What issues have we avoided in our pasts? What issues are we avoiding now?

There is a special reason for the universe giving us 9 months gestation time. This time allows us to iron out our own wrinkles, in time for the baby to get here. If we are consciously aware of the life we are about to give birth to, then we are in a state of emotional and physical preparation.

Everything becomes a factor in the process; finances, job security, clothing, housing, and mental preparation. We have to be concerned about health insurance for either the child or ourselves. We have to be concerned with having a viable income to support a roof over our heads while we embark on parenthood. What is occurring here is that we are learning that we have to provide for this child. We have to create a home for this child to grow in.

Home could mean emotional stability, whereas a parent is capable of providing a stable and loving surrounding for their child, one that will enable them to not be fearful or scared. Or home can mean creating a physical surrounding that houses a family. However, both meanings of home should be united on one level. Not only do you need to provide an emotionally secure foundation for your child, but you also need to provide some level of warmth in housing as a shelter. Does this mean that you must own a home? Or an apartment? Actually, no. Life doesn't always allow us this luxury. However, it is up to you to find a safe place to nest and to grow, even if it is only temporary.

If you are not able to afford your own shelter, perhaps there are friends or family that can lend you their spare room. If you happen to be in this type of situation, know that the universe will provide for you. You will receive what you need as long as you are willing to do the footwork on your end. Footwork meaning that you are focused on creating a stable, emotional home front for your child.

If you are in a poor relationship and the partner is not assisting with this stability then remove yourself from this negativity. Even when a woman is pregnant, the company she keeps in her presence has an impact on her and her unborn. Her baby may even innately trigger physical responses in the mother that will notify her of this negative energy. As a result, the mother may feel extremely sick or emotional when in certain situations or around particular people.

Never doubt the capacity a soul in the womb can have. Pregnancy is a magical occurrence. It is one that can not entirely be explained by medical science. We may know the functionality of birth, but the spirituality is left to the unknown. Only those chosen to experience such a gift and journey can know. The rest is left to observers. What the outside shows is not always what the inside feels. There is much more than what meets our eyes in pregnancy and birth.

From the moment you find out that you are going to become a mother, you will begin this journey of carrying a soul inside of your womb. You learn to nurture your child for the first time, by providing them with a warm place to sleep and to grow. You even begin to make more conscious choices in your life, with your dietary and sleeping habits. So as you are learning how to nurture your child, there is a dual action occurring here, because you are also learning how to nurture yourself.

For some women, being pregnant may be the first time that they take a look at how they treat themselves. Perhaps prior to pregnancy, a healthy diet and consistent eating behavior was not present. Now because the woman finds out she is responsible for more than just herself, she pays attention to these behaviors, and works to correct anything that might have a negative impact on her child.

Through this process of conception to birth, the woman is also learning about herself. The child is not only the student, but also the teacher. It is through having a child that we are reminded to have patience with ourselves. In a round about way we learn as the child learns. We are reminded of the simplicity life has to offer and the comfort it can hold. We are reminded about the responsibilities that we can embody and truly carry out.

We may not always feel confident in our abilities. There will be moments where you doubt your capacity as a human being, and as a mother, or a father, but it is through this doubt that you will discover your own personal security.

Parenting is not a job, it is a privilege. When you are appointed to become a parent you are being given the opportunity to start over where your own parents left off. You are being given the opportunity to either expand on how you were raised as a child, or overwrite their influence entirely. Parenting a child forever leaves an impression and a mark on the universe, so it is a responsibility not to take lightly.

This is your moment of truth when you stand before your Creator and take the responsibility of birth and of life. You are being asked to carry another soul from the spirit world to the earth. The occasion is a very powerful event and marked by preparation on behalf of its parents.

Always keep in mind that you are never given a situation that you are not capable of handling. If you have been chosen to be a parent, it is because the universe has felt that you deserve this opportunity. What you choose to do with this opportunity is entirely up to you. Perhaps you have some things in your life that you need to change in order to accommodate making a healthy environment for your child. Maybe you need to make some career adjustments. Maybe you need to make some lifestyle changes. Now you have a very important reason to do so.

The relationship between child and parent is highly dynamic in nature. You learn together and you change together. You grow into a better person by seeing your world through a child's eyes. The journey of parenting allows us to achieve a new sense of awareness towards our surroundings and the world around us.

Take this moment to assess yourself and your world as it stands now. What do you want to change before your child arrives? Do you have any negative behaviors that need to be addressed? Do you have any poor habits that need to be corrected?

Maybe you are a smoker and have had trouble kicking the habit. Perhaps a child being born would give you incentive to make the change. Maybe you are a drinker, drug user, or an overeater, whatever the habit, take a look at it, for what it truly is. Change begins when we are willing to look at the truth and no longer hide from reality.

Both men and women are prone to anger and depression. If you do experience unmanageable tempers and mood swings, start looking at the culprits before these characteristics affect someone else. Address your emotions before they have negative consequences on you or your loved ones.

Everyone has the ability to start over. Everyone has the ability to change. It is just a matter of assessing your own damage and then going in to make whatever changes are necessary. Paint a picture of the person you want to be and then work towards achieving your vision. Take out your parenting journal and make a section called 'Self Portrait- Now.' Draw a picture of how you see yourself right now. How do you view yourself? You don't have to be a professional artist to draw your own picture, just have fun with it and let yourself go. You can use words or images, whatever conveys who you are right here and now.

When you are finished, take a deep breath and close your eyes for a few moments. Now think of the person you want to become. On the opposite page draw who you want to be. This will allow you to visually see your goals and to see how far away you are from the person you are now to the person you want to be.

For our next exercise, you need to look at what type of parent you would like to be. What is important to you as a parent? Begin by writing down your goals as a parent. Are there any changes that you would have made compared to your own childhood? What did you like about how you were raised? What did you not like about how you were raised? What would you have done different if you were in your parent's position?

It is crucial for us to look at where we came from. Whether we want to acknowledge it or not, that is our foundation. We were given a structure from our birth, however we are not limited to that foundation. We can change the outcome. We can become better individuals and better parental units.

The future is up to us. We can take the 9 months that we have to prepare and make a direction all on our own. Now is the time to focus on the road ahead. Focus on our behaviors and focus on creating a safe environment for our child to be introduced to.

Exercise 1 – Journal Entry

1. Paint a picture of the person you want to be and then work towards achieving your vision. Take out your parenting journal and make a section called 'Self Portrait- Now.' Draw a picture of how you see yourself right now. How do you view yourself? You don't have to be a professional artist to draw your own picture, just have fun with it and let yourself go. You can use words or images, whatever conveys who you are right here and now.

When you are finished, take a deep breath and close your eyes for a few moments. Now think of the person you want to become. On the opposite page draw who you want to be. This will allow you to visually see your goals and to see how far away you are from the person you are now to the person you want to be.

2. For our next exercise, you need to look at what type of parent you would like to be. What is important to you as a parent? Begin by writing down your goals as a parent. Are there any changes that you would have

made compared to your own childhood? What did you like about how you were raised? What did you not like about how you were raised? What would you have done different if you were in your parent's position?

Exercise 2

OPTIONS

Our focus once we become pregnant is usually socially driven. All of sudden, everyone that has an opinion in a 100 mile radius starts approaching us as if they are capable of making major life decisions for us and our baby. All of a sudden, everyone is an expert. Especially if you are a first time parent, you become the target of these "experienced" individuals. It can be rather amusing some of the advice you may start to receive and it can also be rather confusing.

Unfortunately and fortunately this is how some of us begin to learn what type of parents we would like to be. Never forget that at *ALL* times throughout your pregnancy and your never-ending parenting experience, you do have control. You do have options and you do have choices. It is up to you to exercise these choices and to stand up for what you innately feel is right.

Parenting by instinct is parenting by truth. Even if you have never before been subjected to children, you will begin to have instincts on what is right, and what is not right. Some people however, do not have parental instinct. This is usually caused by an obstruction, either physically or mentally, to the adult. If a parent is a drug abuser, alcoholic, clinically depressed, or mentally handicapped, then their parental focus can be blurred. They do not see clearly. Instead of their primary focus being their child and a healthy surrounding, their focus is on themselves, and the unhealthy behaviors they participate in.

Look at being a parent as an opportunity to make the changes necessary to correct your own faults, and move beyond any patterns that no longer benefit you as a person. Having children changes our inner being, and it also changes our outlook on life in general. Issues that did not matter to us before are now beginning to matter. We start to have a different perspective when we realize we are responsible for another human being's life and livelihood.

We have to take care of ourselves. Without us, there is no one to care for our children. We need to feed them, clothe them, read to them, and nurture their spirit's curiosity. We bear the foundation that gives our children the strength to grow. It's not just about us anymore. It's not just about what is good for us. It is about what is good for our family.

You may have tolerated certain life situations prior to having a child, and now that you have a child, you begin to think twice. You may have allowed people to disrespect you or mistreat your presence. Now that you have a family you become more conscious about subjecting your family to any form of mistreatment.

When you have children it becomes a full circle. You give love and receive love. If you don't know what true love is, let your little one show you the way. When they look into your eyes for the first time, you will know exactly real love is as they have the ability to see right through you.

They look beyond any imperfections and they see the truth. Their love for you is untainted. There are no faults at all. Nothing stands between the two of you. There exists only pure love.

Your love for your child begins right now. You are in charge of making the choices that will affect them for a lifetime. You begin protecting your child while they are in the womb. If something is harmful to you, it is harmful to your child. If you are a smoker, you quit. If you are eating food that is not nutritious then you alter your eating behaviors. You make choices now that affect your pregnancy and affect the birth.

When we talk about Prenatal care, we can automatically think about seeking medical treatment. In some instances medical monitoring is necessary. In fact it is quite standard practice among pregnancies. However, there are alternative prenatal care options that one can choose from. It is up to you as a parent to decide what feels right for you and works with your spiritual practices.

Always keep in mind that birth is a natural process. Women have been giving birth centuries before all of the medical interventions were considered mandatory. Obviously these births were successful otherwise we would not have the growth in population that we have today.

Are there complications that occur during the birth process? Yes, but while you are preparing for birth, you must train yourself with confidence instead of doubt. Fear need not be an ally. Worrying about birth and worrying while we are pregnant only causes stress to our bodies and to our unborn child.

Believe in your ability to achieve birth. Remember you and your child are working together to accomplish this magnificent goal. Talk to your baby. Discuss your plans for birth. Discuss your current diet. You will be amazed at the answers that will come to you. The spirit of your child will speak to you.

When we get in touch with our baby we will be given instructions as to what we need to provide it with.

If you are a vegetarian, you may be signaled to increase protein intake or to even temporarily intake meat. Our pregnancy cravings do serve a purpose. What is amazing is that with each child we have, our cravings are entirely different. It just goes to show that each child has its own needs and manifestations that need to take place.

Granted we have to weigh our cravings along with nutritional value. If you crave an abundance of sweets during your pregnancy, try substituting fruit instead of cakes and candies. You may just need an increase in protein to combat sugar cravings. Listen to your body during this beautiful time and learn how to soberly communicate and bond with your baby.

What we are doing essentially is creating an environment for our babies. We are creating a safe home within our bodies so that our babies will be able to flourish and grow. Having a child makes us grow up in the process. We mature with our ideas and concepts to conform to the environment we want to build for our children. For some parents the light switch goes off and for others it does not. You know you are a true parent when your priorities shift to a higher level.

When we begin taking care of ourselves and get ourselves in order, we begin to lay a foundation for our children. Our self health goes hand in hand with our children's well being. What we introduce to ourselves, we introduce to our children. You have to keep yourself in check at all times. Compare the person you want to be to your children with the person you are now.

There is so much activity and change that takes place prenatal. We have nine months to decide if we want to birth naturally or have medical interventions. Perhaps we want a midwife instead of an obstetrician. Maybe we want a homebirth instead of a hospital birth. Some women even prefer having a water birth instead. Don't be afraid to look at your birthing options and make changes.

You may start out with one doctor or midwife and feel that you need to change preference before the child is born. It is okay to do this. This is your right as a mother to make the adjustment based on your intuitions. Some women may not want prenatal care at all. This too, is also your right as a woman. Some women choose to perform their own prenatal care at home. There are many resources over the internet that can be of assistance with this, simply perform a search for at-home care.

Keep in mind that if you do choose to perform your own prenatal care and still give birth at a hospital, you will encounter opposition with hospital staff. Most hospitals are trained to "treat" mothers without doctor or midwife care as high risk patients. Read everything you sign upon admission. This is when your spouse or loved one present at birth will come in handy. During contractions, your focus usually is not on what you are signing, so have your loved one assist you with reading over the fine print.

Also realize that everything you have planned for birth can change at the last minute. Be open to whatever alterations the universe may toss your way.

Maybe you planned a homebirth and ended up having to go to the hospital. Just know that doing so does not mean you have failed. It doesn't matter who gave birth where, it is who gave birth successfully, and both mother and child were healthy during the process.

Assistance with birth is there if we need it. There are a lot of great loving and caring midwives and doctors out there as well as nurses and doulas. Sometimes no matter how bad we want to achieve something alone, the universe asks of us to seek assistance from others. If this happens, look at it as an opportunity to allow someone else the ability to demonstrate their life purpose.

Birth is a beautiful occurrence. Sometimes we are intended to share it with others. No matter how private we wish to be during birth, sometimes the universe asks of us to allow observers. Be open to what the universe asks of you and everything will work out accordingly.

If this is your first child, you are bound to feel that sense of nervousness that a new parent feels. You want to make good choices. You want to make the right decisions for you and your baby. As new parents we only have our influences to rely on. Maybe you have only heard birth horror stories from family members. Maybe most of the women around you have had cesarean sections instead of natural child birth.

It's important to know that you can acquire second opinions to help influence your choices. You may have to go outside of your family members to do so, but you will open up a whole new world of social influences.

As you begin to researching natural child birth and prenatal care, you will see a grassroots underground of natural mothers and parents. You will see other parents questioning prenatal tests. You will see other parents choosing to not circumcise or vaccinate. There are forums, email groups, and an abundance of websites that incorporate natural living along with natural parenting.

Here are some websites that you can reference:

Natural Parenting Magazine

http://www.naturalparenting.com.au/

Natural Parenting Information

http://www.thediaperlady.com/natural-parenting.htm

Mothering

http://www.mothering.com/

Natural Parenting Suite 101

http://www.suite101.com/welcome.cfm/natural_parenting

Attachment Parenting International

http://www.attachmentparenting.org/

Ask Dr. Sears

http://www.askdrsears.com/html/10/t130300.asp

Vaccinating our children has become very common, especially in the United States, as we have guidelines and schedules that are pushed upon us as soon as we give birth. Some doctors will refuse to be your family doctor if you choose to not vaccinate.

Educating yourself on studies and case documentation will help you make the choice that is right for you.

You do have the right as a parent to sign waivers to refuse vaccination even if you are having a hospital birth. Do not allow doctors, nurses, or even certified midwives to tell you otherwise. This is your right as a parent. If you receive any opposition at all, ask them to provide you with a waiver to refuse vaccination. If they ask for a reason, you can declare it as an act out of your spiritual beliefs.

Anti-Vaccination Resources:

Vaccination Information

http://www.thediaperlady.com/vaccine-information.htm

Vaccination Liberation

http://www.vaclib.org/links/vaxlinks.htm

National Vaccine Information Center

http://www.909shot.com/

Vaccination Information Internet Resources

http://www.holisticmed.com/www/vaccine.html

Vaccine Dangers

http://educate-yourself.org/vcd/

Vaccination Laws By State (in the U.S.)

http://www.christianuc.com/vax/law/index.php

Exemption Letters

http://www.christianuc.com/vax/whichexempt.php

If you are going into your pregnancy as a healthy woman then there are little adjustments to make. All you have to do is continue to make healthy choices and your body does the rest. If you do have prior health concerns and you need medical treatment and guidance then do seek a doctor's advice. Medical conditions like diabetes and high blood pressure can drastically change when we are pregnant, so be sure to not take these conditions or any other conditions lightly.

If you feel you are in good health and sound mind and want to perform your own prenatal care then here are some links to reference that will assist you. You can perform your own prenatal care in addition to a midwife or doctor's care. Some women perform their own prenatal care without additional medical attention.

Prenatal Self Care Resources:

Unhindered Living

http://www.unhinderedliving.com/.html

MotheringDotCommune

http://www.mothering.com/discussions/showthread.php?t=496681

C-birth

http://groups.yahoo.com/group/c-birth/

There are several sites and books that have excellent birth stories, attachment parenting advice, and natural health care. Some of the most inspiring books for women are from mothers that have birthed alone or "unassisted." I have been fortunate enough to have met some of these women among some of the communities referenced. Whether you are going to have a natural child birth or unassisted child birth, these books can assist you with mental preparation. They may even inspire you to have an unassisted birth.

Unassisted Childbirth

By Laura Kaplan Shanley

http://www.unassistedchildbirth.com/

Her site has an excellent forum not to mention some very inspiring birth pictures of women catching their own babies.

The Power of Pleasurable Childbirth

By Laurie Morgan

Wise Woman Herbal for the Childbearing Year

By Susun S. Weed

Susun Weed's Wise Woman Herbal for the Childbearing Year is an excellent book referencing herbs that can be used to assist childbearing, pregnancy, and birth.

For women that enjoy coffee normally, but get sick drinking it during pregnancy, you might want to try herbal teas as a warm alternative. You can also try herbal teas that use chicory root that imitates the taste of coffee.

A great herbal coffee alternative is Teeccino, you can visit them at http://www.teeccino.com/. The flavors are all natural and warm your body without all the caffeine.

If you are prone to miscarriages or have any abnormal bleeding during your pregnancy, you should consult with a doctor or midwife before taking any herbs that you are unaware of.

If you are unsure of herbs and whether or not they should be taken during pregnancy, search online and cross reference your resources. If you do not have access to a computer, you can go to your local library and conduct your research on their public access computers.

Here is a general list of herbs to avoid during pregnancy referenced from EarthMamaAngelBaby (http://www.earthmamaangelbaby.com/herbs_to_avoid.html):

Herbs To Avoid During Pregnancy

Many herbs should never be used during pregnancy. Those containing high quantities of volatile oils (some of which could be toxic, such as pennyroyal), or alkaloids, such as barberry, can affect your central nervous system as well as interfere with the development of your baby.

Harsh bitter, such as Mugwort, that strongly stimulate digestion and metabolism should be avoided, as should strong laxatives such as senna, buckthorn, cascara Sagrada, and rhubarb; bitters and laxatives can trigger uterine contractions. Herbs with strong hormonal properties are not advised, including sage and licorice.

Consult your health-care provider if you have doubts about the safety of any herb.

- **Alder buckthorn** (Rhamnus frangula)—cathartic
- **Angelica** (Angelica archangelica)—emmenagogue
- **Barberry** (Berberis vulgaris)—uterine stimulant
- **Birthroot** (Trillium spp.)—uterine astringent
- **Blessed Thistle** (Cnicus benedictus)—strong bitter
- **Butternut** (Juglans cinerea)—laxative
- **Cascara Sagrada** (Rhamnus purshiana)—laxative
- **Coltsfoot** (Tussilago farfara)—possibly fetotoxic
- **Damiana** (Turnera diffusa)—nervous system and hormonal activity
- **Drug Aloe** (Aloe vera)—cathartic
- **Ephedra** (Ma-huang) (Ephedra sinica)—high alkaloid content, cardiac stimulant
- **Feverfew** (Tanacetum parthenium)—emmenagogue
- **Goldenseal** (Hydrastis Canadensis)—uterine stimulant
- **Gotu Kola** (Centella asiatica)—affects nervous system
- **Juniper berries** (Juniperus communis)—possibly fetotoxic, affects kidneys
- **Mugwort** (Artemisia vulgaris)—emmenagogue
- **Nutmeg** (Myristica fragrans) (safe to use in

cooking)—slightly toxic
- **Osha** (Ligusticum porteri)—emmenagogue
- **Parsley** (Petroselinum crispum) (safe to use in cooking)—emmenagogue
- **Pennyroyal** (Mentha pulegium)—emmenagogue
- **Pleurisy root** (Asclepias tuberosa)—cardiac stimulant
- **Rhubarb** (Rheum palmatum)—laxative
- **Rue** (Ruta graveolens)—emmenagogue
- **Sage** (Salvia officinalis) (safe to use in cooking)—emmenagogue, hormonal activity
- **Sarsaparilla** (Smilax regelii)—hormonal activity
- **Scotch broom** (Cytisus scoparius)—cardiac stimulant
- **Senna** (Senna alexandrina)—laxative
- **Shepard's purse** (Capsella bursa-pastoris)—hemostatic
- **Tansy** (Tanacetum vulgare)—emmenagogue
- **Wormwood** (Artemisia absinthium)—emmenagogue

Shepard's Purse which is listed as an herb to avoid is also used by some women towards the last few weeks of pregnancy to assist with preventing hemorrhaging during birth as it is high in Vitamin K. Some women may even use the tincture of Shepard's Purse after birth to slow down bleeding and assist with clotting.

If you want a fun way to ingest Vitamin K, eat more avocados. They have Vitamin K in them naturally and they satisfy a hungry pregnant woman.

If you are also participating in prenatal exams with a health care professional or midwife, be mindful that you are in control at all times. If you begin to feel as though some of the tests they want to perform on you are invasive then you have the right to refuse the procedure. There are waivers for every test you can imagine, so ask to sign one, if your health care professional starts to give you a hard time about refusing testing.

With my first son, I had certified midwives perform my prenatal care along with my own self-care. Some of them were respectful to my wishes and some were not. You will be amazed at how someone can take your test refusal personally.

I began feeling that these prenatal checkups were invasive to my own belief system. I found myself becoming upset going to these visits more than anything. So about four months before my first son was born, I stopped going to the prenatal checkups. I began researching pregnancy and birth even more. If I was going to accept responsibility of my own health, I needed to perform research.

After my initial health screening was performed and the first two sonograms were performed, the other standard medical tests that are practiced were not of interest to me. I didn't want a lot of "checking" of my cervix nor did I want any unnecessary injections. This may or may not be the case for you depending on your situation.

Use your intuition and if necessary seek meditation to find the answers you are looking for. If something with either you or your baby doesn't feel right, then seek counsel either through natural parenting groups, your midwife, or doctor.

With my second child my intuition was extremely strong. Every time anyone mentioned doctor visits or even a midwife, I felt extremely defensive about it for some reason. So I actually never had any care through a doctor or midwife for my second pregnancy. I did however acquire insurance for the birth as I figured if I did not give birth at home, I would need to go into a hospital for the delivery.

State insurance assistance programs are great for young children to acquire as well as pregnant mothers. You can contact your local Department of Family and Human Services to ask how to apply. If you are pregnant and have proof from a midwife or a doctor then they will expedite your application. Your application can even cover medical expenses 30 days retroactive from the time your application was submitted.

About two weeks prior to my second son being born, my water broke. I thought I would immediately go into hard labor like I did with my first son, but I did not. Forty-eight hours had passed and still no signs of hard labor. Everyone was getting nervous, but still I did not want an intervention. My baby was moving. I did not have a fever, nor was there any blood in the waters. Everything was clear. I knew that had I went to a doctor that they would want to intervene and likely try to have me have a c-section. I decided to consult one of the best groups and rejoin cbirth@yahoogroups.com. I referenced their website earlier.

I found out through reading archives and sending out a post about my situation that many other women had broken their waters and still gave birth weeks later, naturally. These opinions gave me reassurance that my intuition was ok. I'm an intuitive woman, but still sensible, so I was certainly glad to have other women share their experiences with me. I do believe research and knowledge are the best backing for an intuitive spirit. It only helps us confirm that our thoughts and feelings are on the right track.

On April 11, 2006, I went into labor in the evening around 8PM. It was hours later that I had contractions minutes a part. By 7 AM or so, almost 11 hours later, still having strong contractions minutes a part, still no feeling of the baby descending. So my husband had called the ambulance, which was our plan anyways, for a quicker admission. Twelve hours later, what a male midwife thought was the head of the baby was really a full bag of water unbroken. Here my body resealed its waters and it was so strong that it had to be broken manually. It was then that I gave birth at 7:11PM to a beautiful, healthy, baby boy, on April 12, 2006, 5 days before my own birthday.

The miracle in this story was that the baby's cord was in a complete knot. If a baby lives through this and is healthy, medical society refers to this as a miracle baby and yes, he certainly was. In hind sight had I had doctor visits and sonograms, they might have saw that the cord was tied, which would have led to the encouragement of an intervention early on in the pregnancy, not to mention a lot of stress, and concerns on my own behalf. So my intuition in this case to not have interventions for my care resulted in a healthy baby and healthy mother.

Prenatal care is the right of a mother to get in-tune with her needs as well as her baby's needs.

Remember it is okay to question normal practices of prenatal care. Research online and visit your local library, and natural parenting groups to find out how to monitor your pregnancy successfully on your own with little intervention from outside sources.

At any time you begin to experience pains or irregular bleeding however, use common sense and seek medical counsel. If you have pushed yourself too much, exercised too hard, your body will find an amazing way to let you know. You may begin spotting or bringing on Braxton hicks. Use your judgment and decide when it is time to relax and take it easy. Don't forget the tremendous task your body has at hand. You need do nothing and your body will still be in motion.

An active pregnancy is important though so don't limit yourself by what you can do. Go for walks, enjoy the sunshine, enjoy your growing belly, and appetite! During my pregnancies one thing I always had to give up was running. There are women out there that do feel comfortable continuing to run during the first 5 months of pregnancy, however I did not feel comfortable with this personally. Excessive jarring on my baby was not something I wanted to endure. Instead I substituted running with walking.

Walking accomplished a lot of things for me. It got me outside by myself, where I could focus and prepare myself for the birth I wanted to have. At times when my husband walked with me, it was a special time for us to enjoy each others company, and explore new territories.

When our hormones are changing, it is important to compensate some of this extra emotional energy that we may have building up inside. Not to mention that when you are pregnant, the world doesn't stop. You still have all the other responsibilities you had prior to being pregnant. You may be in charge of managing your household; cooking, cleaning, caring for your other children, and entertaining them. Some moms have to do all of this and work a conventional or work-at-home job. So walking or performing an exercise that is just for you, allows you to maintain that balance and prepare for any stress you may have to experience throughout your day.

I always viewed my pregnancies as marathons, where it was up to me to train my body, my spirit, and my mind for the birth which was the big race. It was up to me to intake proper nutrients, positive thoughts, and loving energy towards my child. What you feel, your unborn child feels. When you maintain a calm inner being, you create a calm home for your child.

Prenatal care isn't just about our physical state of being, our weight, our blood pressure, or our iron levels. It is about our emotional acceptance of becoming a parent, either for the first time or for the ninth time. It is about us accepting the opportunity to engage in the responsibility of another human being's welfare. Take time to embrace the experience of motherhood.

Talk to your unborn baby. Rub your belly. Play with those little toes pushing through your skin. Embrace the little one and enjoy discovering one another for the first time. Use this time to spiritually work with your own Creator, whatever you may choose to identify with. If you want strength, ask for it. You are essentially working with your Creator when you are allowing a soul to enter your body and prepare to be earthbound. So consider this a team effort between you, your partner, and the universe.

If you are approaching your pregnancy in an already healthy state of mind, then there is not much to alter in your lifestyle, except for monitoring your weight gain, blood pressure, and iron levels. If you were at a normal weight then you will have fewer risks involved. Some women enter pregnancy with pre-existing issues such as diabetes, high blood pressure, or even obesity. Depending on the severity of your condition you may need to consult with a doctor for monitoring the fluctuations of these conditions during your pregnancy.

Being pregnant is intense. Your body requires a lot from you. If any pre-existing health conditions are a concern for you, then use your common sense and seek medical or midwife counsel. If you are entering pregnancy and none of these issues are affecting you then you can proceed with monitoring your health.

Pregnancy is a test on how well you know yourself. For example, I personally have low blood pressure, so when I am pregnant, my blood pressure is only elevated slightly. Being aware of your body before and during pregnancy is the key to a successful birth. Anytime I was out at a grocery or drug store and there was a blood pressure monitor available, I would check my blood pressure. Granted these machines can be off by a few points, but over all it gives you a general idea of your current pressure.

If I was hungry and had an empty stomach, my blood pressure would be a little higher than normal. If I was in a hurry, it would be elevated as well. So I was aware of my body and the affects of situations on my blood pressure levels. During pregnancy we are not only supposed to pay close attention to our baby but also to ourselves.

If we feel sluggish, then we need to ask ourselves if we have got enough sleep. Did we eat enough? Are we consuming the right foods? Are we eating frequent snacks so our blood sugar stays level? Are we getting enough iron?

Be aware of your body's signals to you. Pay attention to your facial coloring. Are you looking healthy? It isn't so much about "prenatal care" as it is about "prenatal awareness." If at any time during your monitoring you do not feel healthy then you need to take an assessment of your actions and your conditions. If something doesn't feel right, consult a doctor or midwife, or natural parenting support group for further investigation.

Exercise 2 – Journal Entry

1. Are you getting enough rest? Are you eating properly? Are you getting enough exercise? Are you exercising too much?

2. What types of prenatal care are you planning on having or are currently performing?

3. Have you performed research that will affect the decisions you plan on making towards vaccinations and if you have a boy, circumcision?

4. What type of influences strongly affects you? Have there been people that have given you advice where their opinions bothered you? What bothered you about them?

Exercise 3
Dietary CHOICES & SUPPLEMENTS

Our diets are an important part of our pregnancy and a variety of habits can be successful. You can eat a raw diet, vegan diet, vegetarian diet, or meat diet and still have a successful pregnancy. You can even eat junk food if you choose to and still have a successful pregnancy. However, there are not a lot of nutrients in overly processed foods. So when in doubt choose fruit verses a twinkie, or carrots instead of potato chips.

With my first pregnancy I was a full blown meat eater. I listened to everyone telling me I need to eat more meat because I was pregnant. Thinking back now, meat always made me sick personally. I was very sensitive to what I consumed. If I had a meat that disagreed with my stomach, I would get sick soon after.

Not to mention meat caused constipation during my pregnancy. Plus I was taking prenatal vitamins that had a huge amount of iron in them.

I started looking towards natural solutions. Instead of consuming tablet forms of iron, I discovered Yellow Dock. I would take that in tincture form in a pregnancy tea made of raspberry leaf, red clover, and spearmint. I would use this tea daily throughout my pregnancy. I increased this from one cup to two cups towards the end of my pregnancy.

The tea helped with nausea and assisted with toning my uterus. The yellow dock provided the iron supplementation that I needed to accommodate my diet. During my first pregnancy I did take the prenatal vitamins prescribed to me by the midwife, however I did not like the way they worked with my body. No matter when I took them I felt sick to my stomach and the high iron content interfered with waste elimination.

Other women will find the exact opposite to be true, they love taking the prescribed prenatal vitamins.

They rave about their hair being thick and nails being stronger, but for other women like myself, I felt these vitamins to be a little too strong for my body type.

With my second pregnancy I took a simple over-the-counter vitamin. I took the same vitamin that I took while I was breastfeeding my first son, so nothing changed for me. I actually continued breastfeeding my first son during my 2nd pregnancy. My body produced milk the whole time which is not typical. Usually at some point your colostrum comes in and replaces the milk, but it did not occur. Even after I gave birth to my 2nd son, the milk was there. I kept expecting it to change over, but it didn't. It just goes to show you how in-tune your body is with your infant and even your toddler while you are breastfeeding.

What is amazing is that with my 2nd child during pregnancy, I was primarily vegetarian except for my 4th month of pregnancy where I had brief encounters with meat eating. I noticed a tremendous difference in my overall health and well-being. With my vegetarian pregnancy, fatigue and constipation did not consume me as much as my non-vegetarian pregnancy. I was not as prone to illness. My nausea was far less and I had more energy. I didn't have to nap throughout the day like I did with my first son.

I felt great. I gained the same amount of weight with both of my pregnancies which was about 30-35lbs. Before I even knew that I was pregnant with my 2nd child I began craving coffee, which was odd because I had gone without it for almost 4 years since my first pregnancy. I kept it under 2 cups a day of course. I wasn't quite sure why I craved coffee, but I did. I later found out that they actually give preterm babies small doses of caffeine to assist with their growth. So who knows, my coffee craving may have been a saving grace for my son whose umbilical cord was tied in a complete knot.

I strongly believe in cravings, I don't argue with them. I may not understand them at the time, but my body's cues are usually for a specific reason. For example, I had been on a vegetarian diet for several years and then one night my unborn child came to me in my dream. This was after I spoke to my baby, telling it to tell mommy if there is anything I need to do that I'm not doing. So that night the male presence came to me and said you are not getting enough protein, you need to either eat more vegetable protein or eat meat.

The next morning I ate a sausage. I ate meat for a couple of weeks and then went back to a higher protein vegetarian diet. I brought eggs and yogurts back into my life. I made soy protein shakes with strawberries and bananas. I ate nuts and legumes. And one thing I craved a lot was avocados. There was nothing like some fresh guacamole, refried beans, and rice.

I later on investigated my craving for avocados and here they are high in Vitamin K. Vitamin K helps prevent hemorrhaging which for a redheaded woman this was ideal. Midwives always note that redheads are prone to bleed more than other hair colors. This is and old wives tale, but one midwives still pass on to one another. It is also something that midwives note to me as soon as they see my red hair.

Regardless, my body was innately telling me what I needed. It was preparing me for the birth. My unborn child was also preparing me for birth by telling me what was needed in my diet so that neither I nor the child was deficient.

Other supplements that I took during my pregnancy were Flaxseed Oil, 1000mg a day. I took this for the Omega3s. I took Evening Primrose towards the last week of my pregnancy to assist with softening my cervix. One herb that I took at the last couple weeks of pregnancy that I had not taken with my 2nd child was Squaw Vine and I wish I had. Squaw Vine is an herb you can add to your pregnancy tea that is supposed to ease birth. With my first son, he just flew out. I had 4 hours of hard labor after my water broke and that was it.

With my 2nd pregnancy I never took Squaw Vine at all and my labor was very long. Squaw Vine is what Indians would brew and intake for easier births. It doesn't taste too good at all, but if you have it with your raspberry leaf tea, you can stomach it.

I always took Echinacea and Vitamin C during time of sickness or if I saw that others were getting sick around me. It always did the trick and lessened my cold symptoms, not to mention it would lessen the duration that I was sick.

I stayed away from refined sugars. Was I perfect at doing this? No. But my body would remind me very quickly that it is not supposed to have junk food because I would get sick right afterwards. Even my healthy chocolate covered raisins would make me sick. Don't get me wrong I tried several times, but each time I would end up with the same result, me hunched down over a toilet.

What else made me feel sick? I don't know why, but toothpaste would make me gag every time I brushed my teeth. I wouldn't always get sick, but it always triggered my gagging reflex for some reason.

That's the beauty of pregnancy. Our bodies just do as they need to. If we let go and don't interfere with the process, our bodies' take over and carry out their duty innately. All we need to do is show up. We need to show up and to listen to what our bodies are trying to communicate to us.

What I needed during my pregnancies may not be what you need during your pregnancy. Every woman and every pregnancy is different. Use this time to focus on yourself and on this amazing ability that your body has. Granted it takes two to become pregnant, but pregnancy is a very spiritual and enclosed moment for a woman. It is a journey into the strength that resides deep within us. Use this time to grow within yourself just as the child within grows.

Exercise 3 – Journal Entry

1. Sit quietly and talk to your baby either out loud or just to yourself. It is best to perform this exercise while nobody is around to distract you. Then ask your baby what it needs. Your answer might not come right away, but it will come. Your baby will know what it needs to do to communicate with you. Your baby may whisper to you or may even come in a dream.

2. What cravings are you having? Are you listening to what your body is trying to tell you?

3. What do you notice about yourself when you are pregnant? What type of experiences have you had or are you having?

Exercise 4

The SOUL WITHIN

We may forget that the unborn child has a spirit already formed. Depending upon your spiritual beliefs or practices will often denote how you view the souls of children. Some view an unborn child as not truly alive until birth. Some believe that the child is alive after 5-6 weeks of pregnancy when the heart starts to beat.

If you believe in reincarnation and the concept of life constantly in a stage of renewal, then you will understand that upon conception, a soul has entered the woman's body and chose to be born into the world. This is where science and spirituality do not always match, so this concept may stifle or challenge some of you.

We briefly discussed the unborn communicating with the parents in our prior chapters, but we did not discuss in depth how willing their soul will go to get their message to us. Pay close attention to the events that begin occurring around you. You may toss them off as coincidence, but there might be much more to it than that.

About a few months prior to our first son being born, I was "nesting' and preparing for the arrival. I made a shrine in the corner of our room. I set up a crib (which by the way I never used with either child). I put on the bedding. I adorned the top of the crib with stuffed animals and toys.

I had a special candle set up on a table along with different items I felt would be a gift for our child. I often spent time in front of that shrine at night praying to my creator, my child, and the universe as a whole. Occurrences would begin to happen after I would go to sleep. Around 3-4:00 o'clock in the morning would be my little ones active time in the belly. (This turned out to also be his active time at night outside my belly.)

My husband would often stay up at these hours working on the computer. Every night around the same time, there was one stuffed animal that would move feet away from the corner of the crib to the center of the crib. My husband would leave the room and then come back to find the stuffed hippo placed perfectly in the center.

So my husband started playing this game with "him" and tried to even trick the little one by almost adhering the tag of the stuffed animal in between the crib guard, and still the hippo was moved into the center of the crib. No matter what my husband did, the hippo would be right back in the middle of the crib every night.

The covers would also move on top of the crib like something was walking on top of them and the crib would creak all on its own. It would only do this during the baby's active times at 3-4AM. The night before his birth, the movements stopped. After he was born the occurrences never happened again.

Another occurrence was that one time my husband was in the kitchen getting something to eat and I was in the living room with my mother-in-law. I had just got done eating some cheese and crackers while I was in the kitchen, but my husband had no idea that I did that. Cheese and crackers was a very common snack for me to have during my first pregnancy.

So I went into the other room and sat down while my husband was in the kitchen. Then he said "why don't you come in here and get your own cheese and crackers, you were just in here." I said, "Honey, what are you talking about, I didn't ask you to get me any cheese and crackers." My mother-in-law agreed I hadn't said anything.

Here he heard a little girl's voice say "cheese and crackers." We had no idea whether we were going to have a girl or boy. The thing is you never know what form the child's soul was prior to being earthbound. You could actually give birth to a boy, but then the presence of their soul felt female because of their prior life experiences.

That is if you accept the concept of reincarnation in the first place. And whether you accept reincarnation has to do with your own experiences and recalls. Some of us are old souls and are triggered by our previous lives so we are able to understand the concept of even our children being earthbound with prior life experiences.

If you are able to make this spiritual connection with your child before birth, they will come to you. Their presence will be felt and made known to you through spirit.

A child's spirit is very clever and playful at the same time. Don't be surprised if they find a striking curiosity in getting their father's involved early on too. Like when my husband would be up while I was sleeping, the closer we were to birth, the stronger the child's soul tried to communicate. It was during these late hours that my husband would actually see the covers on the crib moving.

Granted these experiences are very intense and not everyone will encounter the same type of occurrences, but know that such *little* power can exist.

Our child knew what to do to communicate with us. Your child will know what to do to communicate with you. That is the part that science cannot explain, the communication and bond that exists in utero.

With our second son, he was actually quite excited about entering the physical. He started participating in our lives at 7 weeks into pregnancy. He started doing everything early. He was moving in the belly. Which yes, doctors would say this is not possible, but based on my experience and even several family members feeling the moves for themselves, this baby was moving.

He also found his father quite amusing just like my first son. They have an innate curiosity to see what their Dad is doing. My husband is a photographer and just got a new camera at the time that he was pretty excited about. So he was outside taking pictures at night to test it out. I went outside to check on him on our back porch and then went back in the house. My husband took a picture on the stairs after I was already in the house. That night we sat down to look at the test shots together and the camera caught something we did not.

The camera picked up this floating colorful energy by the stairs where I was standing. It looked like this little embryo surrounded by a rib-like closure. There were no lights on or reflections around that would have caused this. We enlarged the picture at 100% to see the full quality and the details were even more pronounced. My mother-in-law had happened to be visiting at the time so she was able to see the picture too, and she was shocked.

Little instances like this can be rather wild and always unexpected, but they are very valid proof that the child's soul is a very powerful piece of energy. Their spirits are very raw and untouched by our physical limitations. We get stuck thinking that our physical realm is the extent of our lives, that we may overlook the power of the spiritual realm. There is a whole other level of worlds beyond our physical comprehension. The child's soul exists on both of these planes so they can easily perform exchanges from inside the womb and on the outside.

After our second son was born, we also had some other spiritual encounters from another presence. This was an instance that we had never encountered with our first born. We all slept in the same bed together, me, my husband and our two sons. Our newborn would drift off to sleep out in the living room and then I would take him to the bedroom to lie down. Well for weeks every time I would take him to the bedroom he would wind up waking up and crying.

This was getting frustrating for me because I wasn't able to sleep. I kept telling my husband, that I didn't know what was going on. Then one night we discovered what happened. I took our baby in the bedroom, I started to drift asleep, and then the same instance occurred, and our 2nd son woke up crying. So I took him out of the room, walked toward the living room, as to not wake up my husband and other son. As I began to walk out of the door, I heard my husband say, "I caught you, you little shit."

My husband came out of the bedroom and told me what was going on. His hair was standing straight up on his arms and he had goose bumps. He said, I know now why he hasn't been able to sleep and it's because he was getting messed with. I said, "by what?" He said, "by a little boy." He began telling me what he saw. He said that when he heard our youngest boy start crying, he turned over to check on him, and caught the little boy right above him trying to wake him up. When he turned over, the little boy knew he was caught, and chuckled at my husband, and ran off through the wall as fast as he could.

My husband has some spiritual guides that chime in ever so often when they are needed which always amuses me. So when he asks a question, if it something he should know, they are quick to answer. So to himself, he had asked, who was this little boy and why did he keep messing with our son. The guides answered, "It's his brother." And that was all that was said.

My husband had the hardest time telling this to me. He was thinking to himself, how can I tell my wife who just gave birth to our son, that it was his brother. Minutes had passed and finally my husband was able to speak the words out of his mouth and share this with me.

I was just in shock, but glad that I knew what was going on finally. So every night after, my husband had told the child spirit, "It is time to go to bed now, no more playing around." And after that, no more wakeups, our little boy was able to sleep all night. My husband had to be fatherly with the boy spirit and that made him listen.

Was that child our next son? Was that a child of the past? Was that our son's brother in a previous life? That I am not sure of, but it is just another level that is exists in this world that was making its presence known.

As parents we are given the privilege and responsibility of allowing these souls an opportunity to enter the physical realm and learn again, along with adding to our own physical and spiritual being.

Exercise 4 – Journal Entry

1. How are you communicating with your baby? Do you talk to your baby daily? Are you listening to your baby?

2. How is your baby communicating with you? Are you having any spiritual occurrences or changes go on around you?

3. How is your partner communicating with your baby? How is your baby communicating with your partner?

Exercise 5

Positive VISUALIZATION

When we first found out that we were pregnant, I ran out to buy parenting books. I bought your typical best sellers for expecting mothers. I even bought my husband a book for expecting fathers. The truth is that a book can't prepare you for the unexpected twists and turns of parenting. Every child is different and every day is different. You just never know what to expect.

The same goes for preparing mentally for labor. You can do ever preventative test and read every book you can, on what "could" happen during the birthing process, but what it all comes down to is you, your baby, and the universal laws that be.

A successful birth begins in your mind and what you visualize for your birth. We have to remove fear.

We have to eliminate the association between birth and fear, as they should operate on entirely two separate planes. If you are associating birth with fear, then you are essentially telling your body to be fearful of a purely natural process. This can therefore lead to complications and refusals of your body to function on its own.

Whether we would like to think so or not our mental anticipation of birth coincides with our bodily functions. Our body and our mind are a team. One cannot function without the other. When we concentrate on accepting our body's abilities, instead of trying to control them, we allow nature to take over and essentially do what it is supposed to be doing.

The last thing you want to think about are all the "what if's" of labor. You can literally worry yourself sick over occurrences that may not even happen to you. So try to focus on what you want for birth not the "what if's". Focus on what position you want to be in. Focus on your breathing. Focus on your baby.

What we think might happen can actually manifest itself in our lives. If we believe we are going to have a hard pregnancy, then our perceptions may just prove to be right. Our thoughts and emotions towards pregnancy and birth can manifest themselves into reality. That is why we need to spend more of our time focusing on positive outcomes instead of negative.

If we focus on a positive outcome, then we will achieve positive results. Granted the universe will always throw us a few surprises along the way, but we can generally ease our minds during pregnancy, if we constantly encourage our trust in our bodies and ourselves.

Our bodies are so amazing during pregnancy. They have a way of transforming and providing the exact, precise environment to embrace a child. We need only open ourselves to the love we are about to receive and the experience we are about to share with our loved ones.

I had to cleanse my environment when I was pregnant. If there was anything that was going to be negative towards me or give off negativity, I had to rid myself from it. We should be doing this anyways, but granted even I can admit to stubbornly subjecting myself to negative people, especially when dealing with defiant relatives. When you are pregnant though, a protective state of mind empowers you. You discover you don't have to tolerate people with selfish behaviors and motives. All you have to do is maintain a happy environment for your child and for yourself.

The environment is you. How are you feeling? How are you reacting to your life? When you become emotional or stressed that energy is passed on to your child whether you want it to be or not. So it is important to maintain a sense of being grounded even when you are amongst great confusion.

We all want to have perfect pregnancies. We want to be financially sound while we are pregnant. We want to have a safe place for our family to call home. But the reality of life is this doesn't always happen. And in fact sometimes when we are pregnant the universe has a way of doing its own housecleaning.

This is where your spiritual trust comes into play. You have to trust and believe that you are going to be placed wherever you are supposed to be. You will be shifted and tugged in the direction you are supposed to go in. Basically the universe will focus on getting you and your family where it wants you to be before your baby arrives. Some amazing transformations can occur during that time.

You may lose your job. Your spouse may lose their job. You may lose your home, your material belongings. You may have to make some of the most amazing sacrifices along the way, but trust that there is a great reason behind the transition. Expect challenges, and move with the flow, and placement of the universe.

Trust that you will be protected through this transition. Your family will be protected. For all losses there will be gain. The universe has a way of forcing us to make space for the new life surrounding us.

Sometimes the universe sees areas that need improvement before we do, so don't be surprised if some mental and physical housecleanings begin to take place as you are preparing for birth.

Accept your body and accept your environment. Pay attention to all the different insights that are being brought to you. Carrying life inside of your womb is a powerful privilege. It is the magic of a woman. So when you are visualizing your birth, take a moment to focus on how intricate your body is right now. Think about what you ingest spiritually and physically and then visualize this energy passing through to your baby.

What changes would you want to make? What can you do to improve the stability of your body and mind? Focus on your baby. Touch your stomach often. Know that your touch and your energy are being felt inside the womb. Talk to your baby. Include your baby in everything you do. Let this baby know that they are welcomed inside of you.

Along with positive visualization, prayer is also essential. Whatever you believe in spiritually let the universe know that you accept the privilege of being a mother. You are being chosen to allow a soul a chance to be among us again.

Be open. Allow your mind to connect with your child, and ask what it needs you to do. And then listen. Keeping the connection and the lines of communication open will help you and the child have a healthy birth. Your unborn child needs to feel secure upon entering the world. Let them know that you want them here.

As you near birth, feel your stomach more often. Feel every bump and movement. Close your eyes. Visualize your baby's position. Help guide your baby to turn into position when your due date nears. Visualize the baby getting ready to enter the birth canal. Visualize your body hugging your baby and guiding them out into the world.

Embrace your contractions with breath. Take a deep breath in and exhale. Keep doing this with your eyes closed so you can train yourself to react to contractions in this way. Allow your body to work all on its own. Have confidence in the functions your body is preparing to undergo. Know that you need only teach yourself how to react lovingly to the process. You need do nothing but allow your body to do what nature intended. The more you visualize that birth is a natural process, the more you will be mentally prepared to greet your baby. This is a labor of love.

Retrain yourself to remove fear and add confidence. Don't listen to the "what if's," don't listen to the nightmare birth stories, just listen to your own positive visualization of the birth. Repeat this over and over in your head, until you can convince yourself that nothing else exists. Remove fear and add love.

Only you can do this. Doctors, midwives, and friends can provide you with assurance, but only you can convince yourself of a successful birth. It all begins with you. If you view birth as a painful process then that is what birth will be, a painful process. If you view birth as a natural loving process then that is what it will be, a natural loving experience.

Don't spend time agonizing about complications that can occur. If you are doing this then you are doing so for drama not for security. If you have concerns or feel that something may be wrong then go to a professional or talk with your midwife. Stop worry before it starts. Worrying only creates stress for you and stress inside the womb.

You are in control here. Don't forget that. You control what you read, what you watch, and what you choose to listen to. If you choose to listen or be around negativity then that is your own fault. If you wouldn't have your child around it when they are on the outside, then don't surround them with it while they are on the inside.

Our goal here is to have you manifest positivity not negativity. So release negativity and surround yourself with as much positivity as you can. Repel negativity, don't absorb. Reflect negativity, create and visualize a protective shield surrounding you and your baby. When you reflect negativity, you protect yourself from being involved with others behaviors. You protect yourself from contracting bad thoughts or feelings.

Have you ever been around a loved one that was agitated or in a bad mood? Everything seems to bother them. They are on edge. No matter what you say, it is taken in the wrong way. Everyone has bad days. Everyone has days where they get upset and frustrated. This is natural. But when we are around these emotions or negativity, place it in perspective. If someone is not willing to get along with you due to their current state, then perhaps leave them alone before attempting to get involved with their inner argument.

Look at what you own and what they own. You do not own someone else's thoughts or emotions. You therefore have no control over their current situation. You can offer to listen. You can offer to talk with them about what might be troubling them, but it is not up to you to "fix" them or make things all better. So don't take on a responsibility that did not belong to you in the first place.

All you have to focus on is you and your baby. This is a time to be very conscious of your surroundings and your own behaviors more than ever. We are not saying that you can avoid stressful situations, this would not be reality. But you can reconstruct how you view your situations and how you react to daily stresses that come up in your life.

Try to stay focused and try to stay balanced. You may not always get the positive visualization that you envisioned or practiced on, but you can almost guarantee part of the whole will be manifested.

Exercise 5 – Journal Entry

1. What positive visualization do you practice for birth? What type of birth do you have envisioned or want?

2. What negativity do you have around you and what can you do to limit or remove it?

3. What fears do you have about birth? Why?

4. What do you think you can do to rid yourself of any fears? What positive visualization can you replace your fear with?

Exercise 6

Birth & Beyond

You are given nine months for you body and your baby to prepare for the ultimate moment, birth. During these nine months you will have experienced some shifts of emotion from being overwhelmed to feeling such an intense love for your unborn child that you glow with joy.

You will have doubts and you will have moments of insecurity. These emotions and thoughts are very natural. Part of what we experience is hormones and the other part is just normal concerns to have. Pregnancy is a marathon that we train and prepare for as women. We have to mentally give birth before we even get there.

Some of you will give birth unassisted. Some of you will give birth with a midwife present. Some of you will have doulas and some of you will have doctors. The only goal that we can ultimately hope for regardless of how we choose to give birth is safety of the mother and of the child.

Yes we have a lot of medical interventions and even interference, but the good thing about this technology is that it is there as an option. By combining natural remedies along with any necessary medical attention we need, we can achieve successful births where both mother and child is safe.

Some women will not need medical attention, but others will. It does not mean that we are failures as women. Everyone has a right to their own birth vision, but in the end if something serious comes into play during the birth process then know that medical assistance can be sought after.

Even midwife assisted births have back up plans and work with doctors in case of emergencies. It is reassuring to know that in a serious situation if you or your baby needs something to be done quickly then someone will be there to assist you.

Birth itself is amazing. It's the moment we all have been waiting for. It's the big race. It's what we trained for spiritually, physically, and mentally.

During labor the most important thing you can do is focus. Focus on your breath and focus on what your body is trying to accomplish. This is where your trust of your body and the birth process come into play. Work with your body not against it. Know that your baby is working hard as well.

If you are not sedated then your baby will have the energy it needs to kick off of the womb and help push its way out through the birth canal with each contraction.

Our reward is the first moment we get to look into our baby's eyes and welcome them into our lives for the very first time. We hold them and care for them.

We cherish this moment for the rest of our lives. There is nothing greater than this.

You and your loved ones can share this perfect moment. When I gave birth to my first and second son, I just was so overwhelmed with joy and the love I had in my heart that tears ran from my eyes and I could hardly speak. What gifts they were to me. What jewels they were, more precious than I could have ever imagined them to be.

With both of my sons I was able to have a natural vaginal birth. I did however have to have minor stitching performed by a midwife, but only skid marks from the birth, no rips or tares. After the birth, I always felt elated. I was just on a cloud, so ecstatic.

After birth, you then have other decisions to make. If you prepared and did your research, you will have addressed these decisions before your baby's arrival.

If you have a boy choosing whether or not to circumcise them is a personal decision you have to make. This can be very difficult depending on what culture you come from. For Americans it is common practice to circumcise the penis. This is only for cosmetic reasons, however we are told it is for "cleanliness" or to prevent "infections." When you go to have the procedure performed you even have to sign a waiver saying that you understand the procedure is not medically necessary.

However you may have many influential people scorn the mere thought of not circumcising. People might tell you that it is very unhealthy or unclean. Or that the child will have sexual problems later on in life. As a mother you certainly do not want them to have complications as they get older, but let's look at this realistically. Shut out everyone else's perspective or point of view and go out and do your research.

Circumcision was initially common amongst certain religious faiths; Jewish and Islamic religions are a primary example. This form of male mutilation has become routine in the United States over 60% of male infants discharged had reported being circumcised, according to the National Hospital Discharge Survey in 1999. However, the percentage of infant males being circumcised has dramatically decreased from the 1970's reports being as high as 90%.

In other cultures in Africa and in the UK circumcision is not common at all and only performed in extreme cases. Among the Hispanic population in the United States, male infant circumcision is rarely performed. Through education and research about circumcision, parents are increasing their awareness about whether or not circumcision is right for them.

With our first son we had him circumcised. I felt terrible before and after having it performed. At the time I thought that I was doing what I was supposed to be doing for a little boy. After all, my husband was circumcised. His mother circumcised her boys. I honestly didn't know a man that wasn't circumcised. I didn't do the research on circumcision at the time, like I should have. I listened to our primary family influences instead of researching what I felt in my gut. It was our first child and we wanted to do everything "right."

After our second son was born and everyone around me was talking about when he was going to be "circumcised." I had a pit in my stomach. I couldn't do this again. I gathered as much research and testimonials as I could to present my husband with. It just baffled me as to why it was even necessary to have nature tampered with.

If men living outdoors in the wild could have clean uncircumcised penises than surely a little American boy who bathes on a daily basis could have a clean penis without health problems. So after much discussion with my husband and a little opposition from other family members we finally said, "no, we are not going to circumcise." I felt so good about not doing it. I couldn't go through that again. I couldn't have our son go through that either.

Don't be surprised if people have negative reactions when you tell people that you have decided to not circumcise. I've got reactions of people thinking I'm horrible, but in reality I'm only crushing a myth, a myth that we have to perform such an act on our little boys.

Was I concerned about the differences of my husband, my older son, and my little one's penises, my husband and eldest son being circumcised and my youngest boy not? Maybe for a moment the thought encountered my mind, but then that was it. My acquired knowledge on not circumcising an infant male was something I could not deny, only defend.

Don't be afraid to speak up and out about what you feel to your spouse. My husband was very much for circumcision, until I presented him with some facts and details. Here is some research to consider referring to:

Anti-Circumcision Resources

National Organization to Halt the Abuse and Routine Mutilation of Males (NOHARMM)

http://www.noharmm.org/

National Organization of Circumcision Information Resource Center

http://www.nocirc.org/

Doctors Opposing Circumcision

http://www.doctorsopposingcircumcision.org/

When you bring a child into the world, you want to do everything the right way, but you will find out is that what you think is the "right" way, isn't always the "best" way. It is up to you to decipher the difference. Research your options. If something doesn't feel right to you as a parent, research why you feel that way. See if there are other parents out there that feel the same way you do. Join a discussion forum or email group and talk to others that have had similar experiences.

Another decision as parents that you have to make is about vaccinations. If you are having your child at home then you will likely not encounter several common tests or injections that are routinely performed on your child in the hospital. If you do have your baby in the hospital then be aware of "routine" shots and know that you have a right to refuse them.

Both of my son's were midwife assisted births which were great. I certainly felt more comfortable with a midwife than a doctor as I was able to achieve a natural vaginal birth that I wanted without interventions. However, my husband and I did not like the procedures that were being infringed upon us after the birth.

I had done a lot of research about the different tests and vaccinations pushed onto your baby after birth so I knew what to expect, and I knew why I wanted to refuse them from being performed. So before we even went into the hospital for the birth my husband and I were armed with facts about vaccinations that made us decide as parents to not vaccinate our children.

But after our first son was born, we were amazed at how many nurses tried to convince us otherwise. I don't think either my husband or I slept well that first night in the hospital because we were constantly being woken up by nurse's trying to take our baby for "testing."

That was where my husband came in. He was so great at taking charge and letting me rest. They wanted to give our son his first bath. So my husband insisted on going with them which caught them off guard. Come to find out they were going to try and give them his PKU test and vaccination even though we had specified that he was to have absolutely no shots.

The only shot we had permitted was the Vitamin K shot but that was right after birth. We had to sign so many waivers before we left the hospital saying that we denied the vaccines. A lot of parents don't realize that there are waivers you can sign. Some hospitals may try to tell you that you or your baby cannot leave the hospital until certain treatments or vaccinations are performed, but this is not true. Insist on them providing you a waiver.

If they ask you why you wish to refuse these treatments simply say it is for spiritual or religious beliefs. They cannot question that at all. They cannot get children's services after you for refusing vaccinations. It is your right as a parent to not have any tests or procedures performed.

However if at any time your child's health is obviously in need of attention, please do seek medical advice. For example if your child's life is on the line and they have a dangerous fever than yes, seek medical treatment. In case of a vaccination, rethink your options here. Perform your research. Over in China, parents do not vaccinate until the child is at least 2 years of age, as they believe prior to that age, a child's immune system is not prepared to tolerate vaccines.

For us, I knew that we were going to home school our children so vaccinations were definitely not a requirement for us. If you plan on placing your child in daycare, they often request a record of vaccination. Same goes for community schooling facilities.

Pediatricians usually hand you a scheduled shot vaccination list. Government facilities such as WIC and Department of Family and Children Services can even request that your child must be vaccinated in order to participate in certain services that they sponsor. Policies vary in every state so be sure to contact your local agency to check on this.

Even if you want to just wait on having vaccinations administered, know that this is ok too. Maybe you want to get more opinions or do more research. Pediatricians may oppose this, they may even refuse to offer to be your doctor due to this decision and that is ok. If someone is not going to respect your right and choice as a parent with this situation then what other situations may occur on down the line where your parental decision is going to be overlooked? It is up to you to take control and to speak up for your child. Remember you are acting on your child's behalf.

It is your responsibility to find out what is good for their health, not always a physician. If you know the facts before you go into a physician's office then you are the able to make educated decisions for the welfare of your son or daughter.

In this day and time, we have the option to choose a variety of diapering systems. We can use cloth diapers or disposable diapers. With my first son we strictly used disposables. Again, we were influenced by others claiming cloth diapers were far too demanding and inconvenient.

With our second son, months after he was born I started investigating our options. Once I became more knowledgeable about cloth diapers, I had more confidence to take the plunge and use them. However, it took me several months of reading and researching reviews of different brands and options before I actually made the commitment.

Deciding to cloth diaper your baby is one thing, but deciding on what brand is another. It is no wonder so many parents decide on settling for disposable diapers because you just go to the store, make a selection and that is it. With cloth diapers, there are different methods to choose from. Are you going to use chinese pre-folds? Are you going to use an all-in-one? How many do you need to buy? What type of covers do you need to use?

I didn't know where to begin. When you think about using cloth diapers, you typically envision cloth squares that you fold up and secure with large safety pins, but not no more. Cloth diapering has evolved tremendously. We now have the all-in-one diaper that is cloth with a doubler built in the diaper to help with absorbancy. You use that along with a diaper cover and that is all you need. Depending on how heavy a wetter your little one is, you may average using 8-12 cloth diapers a day.

I visited several sites about diapering, but the most resourceful that I found personally was Green Mountain Diapers.

http://www.greenmountaindiapers.com

Here is a great link to get started with your research for new mothers considering cloth diapers:

http://www.greenmountaindiapers.com/newmom.htm

They have a variety of diapering systems available for purchase and they also have a very resourceful FAQ area that will illustrate different diapering techniques with actual pictures.

I bought Bummis Wraps for our diaper covers which average $6-8 per cover, but months later picked up a pack of soft vinyl covers for under $5 for a pack of 6 that are proving to withstand wetness even more than the wraps. You can pick these up at your local Walmart in the infant's section.

Now I only use a disposable diaper at night, but you can opt to purchase an Aristocrats wool cover for nighttime use which is $13-27 per cover. Take time to read everything you can before you buy any diapering system. Also be sure to learn about how to take care of your diapers once you have made the investment as this will prolong their longevity for use.

Other choices that you can make as a parent is what type of sleeping arrangement you want for your child. Do you want to place them in a crib or do you want them to sleep beside you? This will likely depend on how you were influenced growing up. Maybe you were trained to think you had to place your baby in a crib and let them cry it out. Or maybe you always slept beside your mother.

You have to ask yourself if you want to be attached to your child or detached. If you choose to breastfeed then having your little one sleep beside you in the bed is quite convenient not to mention reassuring to your little one.

You goal as a parent is to build trust and to let your child know that they can depend on you for now and for always. Some parents believe placing a child in a crib is beneficial, but others may feel differently. I personally bought a crib with our first son, but we never did use it. I come from a long line of parents that used cribs. I was even cribbed myself.

But when it came down to it, I couldn't stomach leaving my new baby in a crib by himself. He needed me and I needed him. He spent nine months in my womb. He spent nine months listening to the beats of my heart and listening to every breath. Why would I toss him out on his own?

If he began to choke at night, he was right beside me, for me to take action. I felt confident to know that I could check his breathing. I could see if he was cold and needed covered. If he was hungry, he could roll over and hop onto the breast. For me, having this type of sleeping arrangement only made sense. If he needed to burp, I was right there to get him on my shoulder and burp him.

I was able to nurse him and still sleep which is great if you are a new mom. Every ounce of sleep you can get is essential. This also leads in to the choice of whether you want to bottle feed or breastfeed. I knew I wanted to breastfeed my children, but I had no idea how long. I first started out with the concept of breastfeeding for six months then that expanded to a year. After a year I just decided I would do child led weaning. So I still breastfeed a four year old and my newborn son.

We will discuss breastfeeding in more detail in a chapter all of its own. This is a serious choice to consider. Research once again is key. If you know all the benefits of breastfeeding then you will more than likely be determined to breastfeed.

Commitment is essential here. You have to try and research your options, decide which best fits your lifestyle, and then work to achieve your goals. This may or may not cause you to have to alter your life activities, it all depends.

You may have to make arrangements financially. You may have to make career changes. Do whatever you need to do to create the parenting goal you visualized. For example, maybe you are a high class executive, but want to downsize your work obligations so you can be at home with your children. Well, there is nothing wrong with wanting to achieve that goal. If you know you want to do this in advance then you can save up funds and make it a reality.

Life isn't always as neat and clean as that though. Some of us who want to be at home with our children and should be, can have jobs removed from us which are not planned for. Don't worry, the universe will find a way to cradle you and fulfill your needs. You may not be the richest parents financially, but your abundance will come to you in the family you raise. You have to look at needs verses wants, and decipher which is essential for you.

Things to think about are that you are essentially responsible for making choices and decisions on your child's behalf. Work to make educated decisions and responsible choices. You don't have to be perfect.

Parenting isn't about perfection, it is about learning, and the perfect teachers are the children we bare.

At the end of the day, your child may recite their ABC's, but you will take home with you something much more, a lesson of the heart. What you give to them doesn't compare to what they give to you.

99% of parenting is just showing up. Be present. Take the time to embrace every moment. Don't be so hard on yourself either. It's not every day that we are parents. So when the moment finally arrives it can be overwhelming to someone. Just relax, breathe, and be there. Take in the moment and take everything as it comes.

Exercise 6 – Journal Entry

1. What is your after-birth plan? What are your goals as a parent? Do you want to stay at home with your children? What can you do to achieve that goal?

2. What are your views on vaccination and circumcision?

3. What type of diapering system do you plan on using? What are your views with sleeping arrangements?

4. Are you planning on breastfeeding or bottle feeding?

Exercise 7

*Breast*FEEDING

Breastfeeding is an amazing performance from your body. After our child is born, it immediately prepares to nourish our little ones with a natural food that can sustain their growing bodies for a year, and continue to supplement them in years to come.

Your choice to breastfeed or to not breastfeed will depend on what influential mothers you have had around you. These mothers will have either inspired you to breastfeed or inspired you to bottle feed. Or you could always go against their influence and perform the opposite of what they do, which is always welcomed too.

I come from a long line of bottle feeders. Only few of the women around me breastfed and when they did breastfeed they were very discreet about it so I didn't realize how important it was. It was more common to see a Similac container and bottles. I even recall the smell of baby formula, as it was one I always had a hard time stomaching. A lot of preparation was always involved, bottle sterilizing, warming the formula to the right temperature, testing it on the forearm.

What seemed to go along with bottles was a mother not always present, and caretakers being responsible for feedings. Granted if you have to support your family, then this is certainly an option for a working mother. However with the help of modern day conveniences, a mother can also opt to pump her milk and use this in place of formula. This will however require a certain amount of dedication on the mother's part, an investment in a good breast pump, and a cooperative employer.

If you have the luxury of being a stay-at-home mom or work-at-home mom then breastfeeding on its own is a convenient way of feeding your young. It is completely natural and so pure. Your nipples will actually be shaped to fit their pallets the more you nurse. What is amazing as you breastfeed is that you are as nature intended a mother to be, by your child at all times. You are the only one that can feed your child so it requires you to be present, or in distance at all times. Breastfeeding provides more than just milk to your infant. It provides security.

Breastfeeding allows them to know that when they need you, you will be there. It is a very special bond that is established and taught to your young. Not to mention breastfeeding is a very soothing act. It is a time that out of a busy day you have to sit down and sit quietly with your little one. Quiet is certainly a rarity among children so you learn to appreciate these moments.

How often you will be required to feed your little one depends on how much they need. Every child is different and therefore will require different attention to different needs. My first son was on the breast constantly. Even for me to be absent for a shower was sometimes too long. He had very little interest in solid food and did not begin digesting light food until he was about 12 months old. Prior to that, if he ate applesauce it would come out looking the same way it went in.

My son is four years old now and eats a lot of different things, but is still a picky eater. He is also still breastfeeding once or twice a day.

My other son is a tank. He breastfeeds and started taking a deep interest in food at about 4-5 months old. He barks at you every time you eat. He will go at any length to reach for your food. Our first son was the complete opposite.

I breastfed our first son the while I was pregnant with our second son, and surprisingly enough I kept my milk the whole time. They always say that by the 4-6th month of pregnancy your milk will change over to colostrums, but that was not the case for me. So my new little baby didn't have to have the frustration of waiting for the colostrum to switch over to milk.

He had spit up a little on the nurse that was checking his temperature and she was like how is he getting all this milk? My husband and I just chuckled. Our bodies actually identify the stages of growth of our babies and provide the necessary nutrients accordingly. It is this innate communication between your child and the breast.

Your baby's cry will draw your milk down. Just having them sit below your breast prepares the milk to be ready. It is amazing. When your baby is getting ready for a growth spurt, it is like they know in advance, and they begin suckling more frequently. This prepares you to produce more milk to accommodate their needs. According to Kellymom.com, an excellent resource for breastfeeding mothers, "Common times for growth spurts are during the first few days at home and around 7-10 days, 2-3 weeks, 4-6 weeks, 3 months, 4 months, 6 months and 9 months (more or less)." Every baby is different so don't be surprised if they are a little early or a little late with this general timeline.

For a busy person, breastfeeding can take some adjustments because you have to sit down. You have to relax or your milk duct can become plugged. You have to occupy yourself while sitting down for nursing. Some women watch television. Some read a book. Consider this as the universe's way of making you take time out of your day to unwind and relax.

In the past four years, I have spent a lot of time breastfeeding. Being an artist and an author, breastfeeding brought out a different focus in me. I couldn't paint while I was breastfeeding, although there have been moments that I've tried. So I had to develop something that I could do one handed while nursing and that was when I started writing.

You will find something to cultivate your creativity while you are breastfeeding. I can say my laptop computer has certainly come in handy since our children were born. I can pay my bills while nursing. I can email people. I can run a business. I can work on book layouts. I can work on my magazine. I can work. Breastfeeding can fit into your life if you allow it to.

Yes there will be certain things you can't do while breastfeeding, but don't let it stop you from accomplishing the goals you want to achieve. Utilize this experience and work with it towards your benefit. Don't allow it to be an obstacle, instead make it a passage to allow yourself to explore different options you have available to you creatively. Maybe use the time you breastfeed to learn something new. Use breastfeeding to your advantage instead of viewing it as a disadvantage.

Don't forget your body is making food for your baby. So what you ingest your baby will ingest. This means don't smoke, don't consume alcohol, or any illegal substances as this will contaminate your milk. Now being realistic, there are times when a mother can get sick and need medicine. Just be sure to check with your doctor or do a little research online on whether or not it is safe.

Depending on how well your diet is nutritionally, you may want to continue taking vitamins while you are breastfeeding. Your baby's natural iron store is up in 6 months after the birth so you can help your body by taking additional Iron supplements. A vitamin generally has the proper proportion increase of iron that your body needs.

If you begin supplementing baby food you can get iron fortified cereal to help your baby increase their iron level. Your body will eventually get used to nursing and so will you. It takes some adapting. You can't go without eating like you may have done before. When you begin breastfeeding you will actually find you will need more calories then when you were pregnant. If you don't eat enough, your body will slow you down, by making you fatigued. What mom wants to be fatigued? What mom has time for fatigue?

Experiment with food. If something you eat hours later seems to bother your little one, then you know that might be a food you should avoid. My first son was very sensitive to any sweets I ate that were refined sugars. If I had chocolate or anything with caffeine he would be so irritable. My second son is not sensitive to sweets or caffeine at all. Partially due to the fact I consumed coffee during pregnancy. I would have a cup a day. It was one of my cravings.

However, my second one is very sensitive to me consuming milk products. I used to consume yogurts and dairy products to help supplement my vegetarian diet through pregnancy. It wasn't until after my second son was born that he was getting a very odd diaper rash. He would get spots actually around his bum, like a little ring. Nothing I used helped. So that was when I decided to do research and look the condition up on the internet.

It was then when I saw other mothers reporting the same condition and it was pinpointed to dairy products and an allergy to them. I stopped having dairy and his diaper rash cleared right up. It was amazing. It just reinforces the concept that each baby has different needs and sensitivities that we need to recognize.

With my second son breastfeeding, he gets his fill within 10-20 minutes and he is off the breast with an exception on night feedings, where he likes to nurse for a longer duration. My first one would nurse for very long periods. There were times where I felt as though I breastfed him at least 24 times a day. I believe that is what he needed so that is what he received from me.

Breastfeeding is a deep communication between mother and child. It is an unspoken love and nurturing. Not only do the benefits of their health come into play, but there is also a deep sense of security and trust that is established. When we breastfeed we are saying to our child without words, "I am here for you, I love you, Let me nurture and hold you." Breastfeeding has an amazing and calming affect for both mother and child.

As far as preventing sickness, I can certainly say that our first son was very healthy. He didn't have to go to the doctor until he was 2 years old. The first time he went to the doctor was because he had a piece of popcorn in his gums that ended up causing an infection. Other than that, he surpassed flu and colds.

Even if I was sick and had a cold, I always nursed. I would take Echinacea and Vitamin C (*please note this was just personally how I fight off colds, consult a physician if you are unsure of taking these herbs and vitamins). I did invest in Echinacea made with glycerol for my son so if I thought he was getting signs of a cold, I would put a dropper full in his orange juice or herbal tea.

You would think that with me being sick and my son constantly being around me and nursing on me that he would certainly become as sick as me, but that was not the case. My breast milk gave him the immunity that his body needed to fight off the germs that my body was carrying.

You always know when your child is trying to fight off something because they do nurse more. It is as if they know that this will make them feel better. Breastfeeding is a very innate and natural process. When you see the response your child has from breastfeeding you will not doubt nature's gift.

It is very important not to be stressed when you are breastfeeding. Life can toss us many curve balls, but we need to center ourselves and focus on relaxing while we are breastfeeding. The energy you have in your body transfers to your child when you are exchanging breast milk to them. If you have stress within you, you have stress in your breast milk which can cause an anxiety or stress in your child.

There are no doubts that you can feel stressed out before you are getting your little one down for a nap or for sleep. That is to be expected. Getting a child down for sleep usually requires us to face slight opposition, but after they begin to relax, that is time for you to focus on relaxing too. Always take a deep breath in and a deep breath out.

Do something that relaxes you. Read, write, or entertain positive thoughts. Drink plenty of water! If you are getting in to breastfeeding for the first time or even second time, don't forget about water! You will need it. Your body is producing large amounts of milk a day, so your body needs the extra water to sustain your milk and your own fluid intake needs.

Breast milk is widely acknowledged as the most complete form of nutrition for infants, with a range of benefits for infants' health, growth, immunity and development.

-- Healthy People 2010, *Centers for Disease Control and Prevention, Atlanta, Georgia*

According to the Natural Disease Council:

A variety of studies have demonstrated that breastfeeding increases a child's immunity to disease and infection:

- Many studies show that breastfeeding strengthens the immune system. During nursing, the mother passes antibodies to the child, which help the child resist diseases and help improve the normal immune response to certain vaccines.

- Respiratory illness is far more common among formula-fed children. In fact, an analysis of many different research studies concluded that infants fed formula face a threefold greater risk of being hospitalized with a severe respiratory infection than do infants breast-fed for a minimum of four months.

- Diarrheal disease is three to four times more likely to occur in infants fed formula than those fed breast milk.

- Breastfeeding has been shown to reduce the likelihood of ear infections, and to prevent recurrent ear infections. Ear infections are a major reason that infants take multiple courses of antibiotics.

- In developing countries, differences in infection rates can seriously affect an infant's chances for survival. For example, in Brazil, a formula-fed baby is 14 times more likely to die than an exclusively breast-fed baby.

- Researchers have observed a decrease in the probability of Sudden Infant Death Syndrome (SIDS) in breast-fed infants.

- Another apparent benefit from breastfeeding may be protection from allergies. Eczema, an allergic reaction, is significantly rarer in breast-fed babies. A review of 132 studies on allergy and breastfeeding concluded that breastfeeding appears to help protect children from developing allergies, and that the effect seems to be particularly strong among children whose parents have allergies.

Benefits to the Child Later in Life

Some benefits of breastfeeding become apparent as the child grows older. Among the benefits demonstrated by research:

- Infants who are breast-fed longer have fewer dental cavities throughout their lives.

- Several recent studies have shown that children who were breast-fed are significantly less likely to become obese later in childhood. Formula feeding is linked to about a 20 to 30 percent greater likelihood that the child will become obese.

- Children who are exclusively breast-fed during the first three months of their lives are 34 percent less likely to develop juvenile, insulin-dependent diabetes than children who are fed formula.

- Breastfeeding may also decrease the risk of childhood cancer in children under 15 years of age. Formula-fed children are eight times more likely to develop cancer than children who are nursed for more than six months. (It is important to note that children who are breast-fed for less than six months do not appear to have any decreased cancer risk compared to bottle-fed children.)

- As children grow into adults, several studies have shown that people who were breast-fed as infants have lower blood pressure on average than those who were formula-fed. Thus, it is not surprising that other studies have shown that heart disease is less likely to develop in adults who were breast-fed in infancy.

- Significant evidence suggests that breast-fed children develop fewer psychological, behavioral and learning problems as they grow older. Studies also indicate that cognitive development is increased among children whose mothers choose to breastfeed.

- In researching the psychological benefits of breast milk, one researcher found that breast-fed children were, on average, more mature, assertive and secure with themselves as they developed.

Benefits to the Mother

Studies indicate that breastfeeding helps improve mothers' health, as well as their children's. A woman grows both physically and emotionally from the relationship she forms with her baby. Just as a woman's breast milk is designed specifically to nourish the body of an infant, the production and delivery of this milk aids her own health. For example:

- Breastfeeding helps a woman to lose weight after birth. Mothers burn many calories during lactation as their bodies produce milk. In fact, some of the weight gained during pregnancy serves as an energy source for lactation.

- Breastfeeding releases a hormone in the mother (oxytocin) that causes the uterus to return to its normal size more quickly.

- When a woman gives birth and proceeds to nurse her baby, she protects herself from becoming pregnant again too soon, a form of birth control found to be 98 percent effective -- more effective than a diaphragm or condom. Scientists believe this process prevents more births worldwide than all forms of contraception combined. In Africa, breastfeeding prevents an estimated average of four births per woman, and in Bangladesh it prevents an estimated average of 6.5 births per woman.

- Breastfeeding appears to reduce the mother's risk of developing osteoporosis in later years. Although mothers experience bone-mineral loss during breastfeeding, their mineral density is replenished and even increased after lactation.

- Diabetic women improve their health by breastfeeding. Not only do nursing infants have increased protection from juvenile diabetes, the amount of insulin that the mother requires postpartum goes down.

- Women who lactate for a total of two or more years reduce their chances of developing breast cancer by 24 percent.

- Women who breastfeed their children have been shown to be less likely to develop uterine, endometrial or ovarian cancer.

- The emotional health of the mother may be enhanced by the relationship she develops with her infant during breastfeeding, resulting in fewer feelings of anxiety and a stronger sense of connection with her baby.

- A woman's ability to produce all of the nutrients that her child needs can provide her with a sense of confidence. Researchers have pointed out that the bond of a nursing mother and child is stronger than any other human contact. Holding the child to her breast provides most mothers with a more powerful psychological experience than carrying the fetus inside her uterus. The relationship between mother and child is rooted in the interactions of breastfeeding. This feeling sets the health and psychological foundation for years to come.

Social and Economic Benefits of Breastfeeding

The benefits of breastfeeding go beyond health considerations. Mothers who nurse their children enjoy social and economic advantages as well. For example:

- Women who breastfeed avoid the financial burden of buying infant formula, an average expense of $800 per year.

- Breast-fed babies are less likely to need excessive medical attention as they grow. In one study, a group of formula-fed infants had $68,000 in health care costs in a six-month period, while an equal number of nursing babies had only $4,000 of similar expenses.

Breastfeeding in the Unites States of America is very low in numbers unfortunately compared to other countries. According to the 2002 National Immunization Survey, the following statistics were documented:

Results. More than two thirds (71.4%) of the children had ever been breastfed. At 3 months, 42.5% of infants were exclusively breastfed, and 51.5% were breastfed to some extent. At 6 months, these rates dropped to 13.3% and 35.1%, respectively. At 1 year, 16.1% of infants were receiving some breast milk. Non-Hispanic black children had the lowest breastfeeding rates. Breastfeeding rates also varied by participation in day care or the Women, Infants, and Children program, socioeconomic status, and geographic area of residence.

Conclusions. Although the rate of breastfeeding initiation in the United States is near the national goal of 75%, at 6 and 12 months postpartum the rates of breastfeeding duration are still considerably below the national goals of 50% and 25%, respectively. In addition, rates of exclusive breastfeeding are low. Strenuous public health efforts are needed to improve breastfeeding behaviors, particularly among non-Hispanic black women and socioeconomically disadvantaged groups.

(* Online Resource:
http://pediatrics.aappublications.org/cgi/content/abstract
/115/1/e31?etoc)

Sadly enough, some states in the U.S. have only recently made breastfeeding in public spaces legal. According to the National Conference of State Legislatures, November 2006 reports, only 21 states have declared breastfeeding exempt from public indecency laws:

Alaska, Arizona, Florida, Illinois, Kentucky, Michigan, Mississippi, Montana, Nevada, New Hampshire, North Carolina, Oklahoma, Rhode Island, South Carolina, South Dakota, Tennessee, Utah, Virginia, Washington and Wisconsin

36 states have laws written specifically allowing women to breastfeed in any public or private location:

Alabama, Alaska, Arizona, California, Colorado, Connecticut, Delaware, Florida, Georgia, Hawaii, Illinois, Indiana, Iowa, Kansas, Kentucky, Louisiana,

Maine, Maryland, Minnesota, Mississippi, Missouri, Montana, Nevada, New Hampshire, New Jersey, New Mexico, New York, North Carolina, Ohio, Oklahoma, Oregon, South Carolina, Utah, Tennessee, Texas, and Vermont

Breastfeeding is such a natural occurrence. It is baffling to think that some people may view it as unnatural or even indecent. Yes, it does take time and dedication on a woman's part. You can't just breastfeed one day and not the next. You have to be committed and most important, you have to be present.

There are organizations to assist you with breastfeeding and to share your experiences with if you have concerns. La Leche League International being one of the most active organizations in the world. (http://www.lalecheleague.org) You can contact your local group and attend meetings if you so desire. Usually if you are birthing in a hospital, you will have a La Leche League Representative on hand to assist you with any help you may need or to answer any questions you have about breastfeeding.

A lot of women are concerned with getting that first "latch" on to the breast. If you just relax and let your baby innately take over, you will see that this isn't too much of a concern. They know immediately where the food source is. It is amazing. They come out of the womb and just know exactly what they are supposed to do. On rare occasion will the baby be confused.

Remember your own energy affects your baby's energy. The more relaxed you can be about breastfeeding, the more relaxed your baby will be. The more confidence you have when you breastfeed, the more confident your baby will feel.

Breastfeeding does not hurt. If it does hurt you, then you need to make sure your baby is breastfeeding properly, and has the whole nipple inserted into the mouth, not just the tip. If they are not latched on properly, gently place your finger in their mouths and release their suction, and then re-latch them back onto your breast.

Take care of your breasts. They are performing a great function here. Do not use harsh soaps on your breast when bathing. You don't want to dry out your nipples as this will cause them to be sore and crack. Generally washing them with just hot water alone keeps them freshened up. When you first begin breastfeeding, you milk "let downs" can feel odd. It is usually just a slight tightness. This is nothing to be worried about as your body is doing exactly what it is intended to do.

You will often leak out of the other breast while your baby is nursing off the opposite one. You can use a towel to place under the leaking breast to prevent your little one from becoming wet. Leaking should subside after your body becomes adjusted to breastfeeding usually around 6 months. However, I always have leaked, it just stopped projectile spurting after 6 months.

My boys and family members call the rags we use for these leaks, "tit-tit" rags. I always have a towel in reach, especially when I am in the bed. When you breastfeed at night, you may want to prepare your bed.

We use a waterproof cover over our mattress to prevent any milk from soaking into our mattress while we sleep at night. You can also buy just a waterproof crib mat and place that under your sheets too.

You will want to invest in at least two good nursing bras. However, with my first child, I nursed so frequently that I never wore a bra at all. Some of the nursing bras I had tried were your standard nursing bras you get in the department stores. They were too tight and caused my breasts to get engorged and my milk ducts to get plugged. So I ended up avoiding them altogether.

With my second son, I was able to go online and find two good bras that I could use. They were a more expensive than the other ones, about $20 a piece, but they work great, and are sturdy for me to use. Depending on how large your breasts are, you may need to always where a bra to compensate for the heaviness your milk creates. If you are going to wear a bra all the time you need to make sure you get the right size.

I still have trouble accepting reality of my breasts being larger than what they were pre-pregnancy. So it is easy to shop for your old bra size verses what your new bra size is. After your milk has come in, measure your breasts to find out what your new bra size is. If you don't have seamstress measuring tape, you can just take a string or piece of yarn and measure yourself that way. Then place the string length on a ruler or industrial tape measurer.

According to an article on KidsHealth.org, here are standard tips on measuring your bra and cup size: (http://kidshealth.org/college/your_body/take_care/bra.html)

Chest measurement: *Bra fitting experts offer two methods of calculating the chest measurement. The most common method involves running a tape measure just under your breasts, all the way around your back and rib cage. The tape measure should rest flat on your skin and lie straight across your back - not so tight that it digs in, but not so loose that it sags down in back.*

Make a note of your measurement and add 5 inches. That's your chest size.

You can also estimate your chest size by running a tape measure across your chest above your breasts, under your armpits, and around your back (measure from the same back position as in the first chest measurement option). This method is easier because you don't have to do any addition or other calculation, but some people feel it's less accurate than using the first method.

If your chest measurement comes out as an odd number (such as 31 inches or 33 inches), it's usually a good rule to round up to the next number. Most bras have a few sets of adjustable hooks and eyes, so you can adjust the tightness. It's a good idea to round up, rather than round down, because when you buy a new bra that hooks on the first or middle hooks - rather than on the last - you can leave room for stretching.

Cup measurement: *As with the chest measurement, when you're measuring for cup size, make sure the tape is snug - not too loose or too tight. If you already own* an unpadded bra that fits well, wear it when measuring for cup size. Avoid using a sports bra, which can flatten breasts and give a cup reading that's too small.

This time, when you run the tape measure around your body, you're going to take the measurement across the fullest part of your breasts. Write down this number. Now subtract your chest measurement. If the difference between the two numbers is less than 1 inch, your cup size is AA. If it's 1 inch, your cup size is A; 2 inches, you're a B; 3 inches you're a C, and so on.

So you've taken your measurements and you're in the fitting room trying a bra in what's supposed to be your size - but it doesn't seem to fit. Now what? Before you pile on all your clothes just to go out and look for a different size, experiment by making some adjustments to the bra. Extend or shorten the band around your chest slightly by moving the hooks to a different eye on the hook and eye closure (or adjust the velcro if the bra has a velcro closing). The bottom band of a properly fitting bra should ride across the middle of your back and pass under your shoulder blades to provide the right support.

A bra's straps allow you to modify how the cups fit and support your breasts. When the straps are the right length, a bra lifts the breasts comfortably and the back of the bra will run straight across your back (if a bra is pulling upward in the back, it may be a sign that the straps are too tight). You should be able to get one finger under the straps to prevent them from digging into your shoulders. In general, women who are petite will need to wear their bra straps shorter than those who are tall.

Don't be surprised if your little one favors one breast more than the other. My right breast produces more milk and is larger than the left. For some reason when my milk came in for the first time, it produced more on the right side than the left side. So there is a size difference now. No matter what the baby's preference is though, be sure to switch breasts to keep milk production even in both breasts.

You might forget which breast you left off on. Some women come up with ways to remind themselves by wearing rings or bracelets on a certain hand and then switching the item to the other hand. I always just felt the one breast to measure how much milk was in the breast. If one breast was tighter than the other that usually meant that it was ready to be nursed on. You will begin to innately switch breasts. I do so in my sleep. I will switch my baby from side to side without even thinking about it.

Breastfeeding is very rewarding and also hilarious at times. It is so amazing how these little ones with their eyes closed can search for the breast and root for it. The smell alone they rely on. Sometimes they can be a little off target too if it is at nighttime, that's when you might be awoken by a power hicky.

Breastfeeding is a comforting way for your little one to explore their new world. Watch how they investigate their surroundings behind the security of your breast. They will watch and study unfamiliar faces and places.

When you first begin breastfeeding you might be a little shy about breastfeeding in public places, but after doing it for a while you certainly get over it. With my first one, I was breastfeeding constantly, so it was very difficult to go anywhere without having to face the fact that I would likely have to breastfeed out in public.

Yes, I would certainly get many different reactions and stares, but I would just block it out and continue to take care of my feedings. If we were near our vehicle, I would just go in there and breastfeed. If I was at a restaurant and could do a feeding discreetly I would just place a blanket over my infant and breastfeed there. As they get more curious, the blanket trick doesn't seem to work. They end up fussing until you remove the blanket which doesn't help you be discreet.

So then I would either have to go into a bathroom stall and breastfeed there, or go out to our vehicle. When they are real small in the first few months breastfeeding in a store or out while you are walking is no big deal. Again this all has to do with what type of person you are, and how comfortable you are with breastfeeding. Some women insist on not being seen when they are breastfeeding and that is fine. Others integrate it into their daily activities and tasks. Some women place their babies in a sling and are able to be very discreet. However, I tried a sling with both of my boys and they did not like it at all. They were too curious to be covered up.

If you are willing to be out in public breastfeeding, know that you are doing a very large service to young girls everywhere. When I am out breastfeeding, granted I get many stares from men, but I also get curious stares from young girls and women. Maybe they have never seen someone breastfeed and maybe, just maybe, the concept might catch on.

One time we were over a relative's house and the boy there was around 10 years old. He walked in the living room not knowing I was breastfeeding my son, and he had no idea what I was doing. I was amazed at his curiosity. He was immediately taken into the other room by his grandma and mom, but that didn't stop him from asking questions. He wanted to know what I was doing. So his mom explained, "She is breastfeeding and giving her little boy milk." His next question was, "was I breastfed?" The mother replied, "No, you were bottle fed." The boy then said, "why didn't you breastfeed me?"

The conversation was rather interesting and just goes to show you that you don't have to be ashamed of breastfeeding. Do it and be proud of it. Maybe some day the people that witness you breastfeeding will have a curiosity to do it themselves when they have families of their own.

I'm not saying you have to have your breasts dangling out there for the world to see, as you will learn a technique when you are out in public, to keep them concealed. A lot of women might rely on pacifiers especially when they are out in public to calm the child's need to breastfeed. For me personally, this was not a tool that I used. Granted there are many families that will disagree with me there and that is fine.

I was very adamant about not using pacifiers. I just innately felt that it might prevent the child from expressing or communicating their needs to us. If they were hungry I wanted to know it. I didn't want them to be fooled that they were receiving nourishment just because their suckling was satisfied by a pacifier. I also believe that not using pacifiers assists them with their speech development. When their mouths are not being occupied by a pacifier, they are more apt to make noises and formulate syllables.

Does this mean you will hear more noise? Yes, it certainly does, but it allows you to know what your child needs, and it teaches them to communicate those needs to you. Especially at night time, they suckle when they are hungry, so they look for the breast not for the pacifier. The more frequently they breastfeed, the more milk you produce.

I ran into a lot of opposition about not using a pacifier. I had family members insist that my children needed one and they would even keep several around the house "just in case I changed my mind." Even the hospital wanted to shove a sugar water dipped pacifier in our son's mouth while they ran tests. We allowed a pacifier to be used once during a hearing test but that was it.

If you do decide to breastfeed know that you are making a commitment to your baby that will benefit them for years to come. Not only are you providing them with love and nutrition, you are providing them with security and growth. Consider your options. If you have to make life adjustments to breastfeed then do it. Don't be afraid to use what nature has given you. Breastfeeding is a privilege that you as a woman are being allowed to enjoy and experience.

Exercise 7 – Journal Entry

1. Have you ever breastfed your children before? If so, for how long?

2. Do you have any fears about breastfeeding? Do you have any mental inadequacies about breastfeeding that need to be addressed?

3. Were you breastfed? Did you see others around you that were breastfed? What are your perceptions on breastfeeding?

Exercise 8

Balance

Parenting can take a lot out of you, but what we receive in return from our children, is more than what we could ever ask for. You wouldn't imagine your life without them. Children expand our minds, and challenge us to develop new perspectives on our own surroundings, and the world as a whole.

But being a parent requires us to balance and perform many tasks at one time, especially if you have more than one child. Once your children begin to vocalize their requests, you will then realize how many tasks will be asked of you simultaneously. You will have to change diapers, wash clothes, get them dressed, make breakfast, lunch, and dinner. You will have to challenge them and entertain them. You will have to mentally and physically stimulate their growing quest for knowledge.

And yes, you will be asked to do this while still taking care of yourself in the process. This is where balance comes in. In order to be a good parent, you have to still take care of yourself. You have to still do things that you enjoy doing too. That's not always an easy task. A lot of us have to work 40 hours or more a week to financially provide for our family and after that 40 hours is up, we are responsible for the other demands that our children may have for us, not to mention the dedication we owe to our spouse or partner.

Time management certainly becomes a factor. We can feel like there is not enough time in the day to accomplish everything we want to accomplish. When we do get some down time from our parenting responsibilities, it is important to use that time to do something for ourselves. This down time is usually during a child's nap or when they go to bed at night. Maybe you want to read. Maybe you just want to sit down and relax. Whatever it is that you want to do, just take that little bit of time that you do get, to do it.

Everyone needs to recharge. If we don't, then we are just left exhausted and our energy is depleted. Do something during these rare quiet moments that allows you to relax and unwind. These moments will enable you to deal with all the other demands that being a parent has to offer.

We always have moments when we worry about our children. Maybe they don't feel good, maybe they seem sad, or maybe something is bothering them. Worrying can sometimes feel like a full time job. Some parents may have special needs children which may make their lives even more challenging. Or maybe your child has health issues that require a lot of attention.

No matter what the situation may be, it is important to understand that worrying about issues that are beyond our control, can overly consume our world. Know that taking some time to focus on yourself no matter what difficult circumstance you might be facing is not a selfish act.

Having an outlet is very important. Maybe you have a creative outlet you are neglecting. Maybe you just need some special time to take care of yourself. After you have children even taking time out to take a shower can be a challenge. Your life gets flipped upside down, it's amazing. One moment you have free time and the next minute you are trying to adjust your responsibilities to work free time in.

So if you are a first time parent, making these changes can be a challenge. If you are second time parent, you are apt to be more accustomed to the pace and the responsibilities of having a child. So the other child adds to the fun. It also makes it even more challenging to find that balance with your responsibilities with others and your responsibility to yourself.

The goal of parenting secretly is that we are able to get closer to ourselves than we were before, not further away. Parenting expands the way we look at the world around us. All of a sudden things that didn't matter before, matter to us now. We remove the blinders and see the world as it is. We may see the dangers and the ills of society, where before we did not. Now that we have children, those dangers begin to concern us. Now we want to make a difference. We want to make the world a better place for ourselves and for our children.

So having time to ourselves to think about our roles and involvement in the world is essential. If you want to get somewhere in life, you first need to look at where you are, and then figure out where you would like to be going.

Being a parent means that you are a foundation by which your child will base their own inspirations from. If you have a strong foundation then your child will acquire strong attributes. If you have a weak foundation then your child may inherit weak attributes as they get older. Does a strong foundation prevent our children from making poor choices as they get older? No, not at all, but having a strong foundation provides them with a ground to stand on and a life example to seek out.

The key with someone maintaining a strong sense of foundation is through balance. For example, if you work too much, then you are taking away from other areas in your life, family being one of them. Most of the times children don't remember the fact that you worked two jobs to support them, they remember that you weren't there to be with them. The most important thing to a child is your presence.

So keep that in mind when you over extend yourself at your job. Are the extra hours and time you put in to your job really worth the sacrifice? We need to be able to have money for food, clothing and any extra amenities, but can we alter or adjust our lifestyles so that we can maintain our finances and *our* family? The work-family balance is our challenge.

The best way to figure out your current equation is to assess where you are at right now. Get a sheet of paper out and write down how many hours you spend working at your job or in your home a day, then calculate how much time you spend with your children a day, and how many hours you spend with your spouse. Then calculate how much time you dedicate to yourself a day.

The role of balance is no easy equation at all. It is a challenge and it seems that every day can be different and fluctuate as some days we need to focus on one area more than the other, but if we constantly keep our life responsibilities in a rotation then we can make that balance a reality.

Our children are not going to be young and little forever. They will soon grow up and not require as much attention as they did before. So it is important during these priceless moments that we allow ourselves to savor the time spent with our children; reading, playing and just being together.

We cannot guarantee that every day we will have balance in our lives, but as long as we keep the concept in our minds, we will remember to strive for such a goal. Your ability to balance, your life, your work, and your family, will also make an impression on your loved ones around you.

Be an example. Be the one that stops to think about their choices and decisions. Are you going to invest time pleasing your friends? Or are you going to spend time being with your family? Ask yourself what the balance is between the two. Are you going to focus on pleasing your boss and spend extra hours at work? Or are you going to spend your time wisely?

Money and time are always a factor. Sure who doesn't need or want a few extra dollars at the end of the week? But listen to what you are saying and identify whether it is a need or a want. Is it a necessity to work the extra hours? Are you in danger of losing your housing shelter? Are you in danger of not having food? Put reality into perspective and negotiate with yourself over the benefits.

The same goes with our love relationships. Our new role as parents doesn't cover up the roles you have with your partner. We still need to have couple time. Granted it may not always be convenient or feasible, but when you do have time, take it together.

Sometimes it is hard for couples to even communicate with one another around their children. Especially if you have one or more children present in the home. Once those babies start talking, they don't stop. Try to use alternate forms of communication with your partner or spouse. If you both work on your computers, install a chat messenger so you can keep connected. You can send emails to each other too.

If you are not both on a computer then maybe write little notes to each other here and there. Whatever you can do to let your loved know that you are there for them, do it.

There is so much demanded of us when we become mothers that by the end of the day, we are merely exhausted. We hit the bed and we are out. It is a difficult adjustment sometimes for our partners to realize how much attention is required by our little ones, that our partner can begin to feel left out.

It's important to let them know they are still a valuable asset in our lives. We need them to love and support us in parenting as well as our partnership together. Some people are chosen to parent alone and that is also ok too. The universe gives us the tools that we need to overcome situations, to work with what we have, to make and support a life for ourselves and our children. Whether you have a partner in parenting or not, doesn't make you love your child any more or less. However, if you do have a partner present in your life, keep in mind to always make them a priority too, along with your children.

Relationships do take effort and we have to be able to meet our partners half way. We have to be willing to understand their perspectives, acknowledge them, and then work to make a successful compromise.

We have discussed our balance with loved ones, with our jobs, and with ourselves so that adequate time is dedicated to all areas of our lives. Another area of our lives that requires balance is when we overdo ourselves as a parent. Some people are on the opposite side of the spectrum and are "too" good of a parent.

When we focus too much on our family or our children other areas of our lives can go deprived. Maybe our work is suffering because of our lack of concentration. Or maybe we ourselves are suffering because of lack of sleep and care for ourselves. Sure our family may be thriving, but we may have exhausted ourselves in the process.

The best thing we can do is step back. Focus on a time in your life where you felt you were the most successful. Maybe this point in your life you were active in sports or dance. Maybe your career was thriving. Now focus on what your appearance was at this time. Was your weight balanced? Was your image balanced? What was your self esteem like at that time?

When we go forward in our lives, there are some areas that may have taken a step back. Things shift when we become parents, there is no doubt about that. Maybe prior to having children, we would never step foot out of the house, even to check our mail if our makeup wasn't on or hair wasn't done, but now that we have become parents, we are willing to go outside in our pajamas with our hair tucked up in a pony tail. Everyone has their own scenario that they can reference. Our children and our family become such a focus that we ourselves were left waiting for a recovery.

This is normal. However, there does come a time when we need to reclaim ourselves. We need to take a moment to remember our successes, and do what we can to achieve self improvement right now. Maybe this means starting an exercise routine. Maybe this means going for walks. For some people maybe this simply means waking up and showering and getting dressed for the day.

What we do for ourselves, we are ultimately being an example for our children, and our family members. You may feel guilty for taking time out to spend on yourself, which is normal. We become so focused on our family, or our children, that the blinders we have placed on ourselves, may not let us see what we look like below. Is our body in shape? Are our minds in shape? Are we achieving our goals? Or have we set aside everything to focus on our family?

When we become parents we are limited on some of the things that we used to do. But it does not mean that we have to give up on ourselves. We simply have to find more creative ways of achieving these goals and go forward. Don't give up at the first signs of struggle. That will only lead to frustration and then guilt for never achieving what you set out to achieve. Work your goals into your lifestyle and eventually others will get accustomed to your success, even you.

Set realistic goals for you to achieve daily. Maybe you just want to get 10 minutes in for a walk, or maybe you want to spend 10 minutes doing something that means taking care of yourself. Whatever you want to accomplish, take baby steps to get there. If you learn to practice taking these steps daily, it will soon become a positive habit that you have developed.

Your partner or spouse may look towards you as an example of what they can achieve themselves. Add a little spice to your life and start putting something new on. Maybe get yourself a new shirt or wardrobe. Even though you are a mom you are still allowed to be yourself. You are allowed to buy things just for you. You are allowed to do things just for you. You don't have to wait until your children get older. You can do things right now, even if it is something so simple. You can do things right now for yourself.

Achieving balance in our lives is an ongoing process, so be patient with your self. Don't get frustrated if at first you don't succeed. Adjustments and change can be difficult for both the people initiating the change and the people around them. Don't be surprised if you encounter resistance from those impacted by your lifestyle change.

Those who truly love, honor, and support you will continue to do so. For those who were merely along for the ride, you may shed their presence and necessary weight. You don't need negativity in your life, you need support.

Balance takes courage and devotion. We have to have the courage to make changes in our lives and know that we are building upon our own foundation.

Making changes and becoming devoted to those changes is very crucial. Follow through with your goals. Listen to yourself and listen to the spirit world that guides you. Partake in this journey and you will partake in a life long lesson learned.

Exercise 8 – Journal Entry

1. What areas in your life do you feel need to be balanced?

2. Set aside a section in a notebook and write down what you spend your time on in a day. Estimate the hours spent with your children, spouse, yourself, and any work you perform in and out of the home.

3. Once you have completed your assessment, take a look at what areas in your life you spend the least amount of time on. What areas need improvement? What steps can you take to make a conscious effort on managing your time more effectively?

Exercise 9

Lifestyle PARENTING

Parenting varies and depends on the influence surrounded by the parent or parent(s). It can also differ based on culture, background, spiritual beliefs, or socio-economic factors. One thing that unites us in our concept of parenting is that parenting becomes a lifestyle. If you are a full-time parent then you know that when you embark on this beautiful journey, you are embarking on a lifestyle transformation.

Parenting is not a cloak that we can take on or take off. It is a metamorphosis that occurs in our lives and our relationships. It forever places an impression on our hearts. Parenting is also a unique form of care which is based on style and technique. We could all read the same books on parenting, but parent our children in an entirely different way then what the book instructed. Parenting is not something that is black and white.

Every child is different, therefore every parent is different. We may have guidelines or principles that are followed, but our parenting will always be suited to the needs and requirements of the individual child. Our children fit into our lifestyles and we fit into theirs. Our goal is to integrate our children into the things we love.

If we look at the big picture and put on our spiritual scopes we can see that the children we were given were for an exact and precise purpose. There are no accidents with births. Each one has a purpose. The child and universe chose you to be their parents. You possess what this child needs to learn their life's lesson.

It's not just what we teach our children during the day, it is what we teach them overall in a lifetime. This is not to say that a child born to a carpenter will become a carpenter. Instead the child born to a carpenter and a homemaker will combine the skills of their parents and integrate them into their own lifestyle, their own concepts of life.

The universe is very intricate with the spiritual details of parenting. What is amazing is children encounter so many different scenarios with their parents. Some may have different birth parents. Some may not know one of their parents. Under these circumstances consider how much effort the universe had to undergo to create the ultimate life lesson for this child.

Instead of having two parents the child essentially has four, two for the birthing and earth entry, and then two others for the duration of the child's life. When we view life situations in this manner then it is perhaps easier for us to understand why some circumstances happen.

What you have right now is what you need for this moment and this moment alone. Each day you will acquire new tools and new strengths to therefore extend to your loved ones and to your children. Your gift to them is the life you lead.

Life isn't always what you think is "perfect." But know that your idea of perfection can be quite different from the universe's idea of perfection. Sometimes the right conditions in our life need to be created in order for the appropriate outcome to take place. The right conditions may feel wrong or out of sequence, but have courage and strength to believe that there is always a lesson nestled in the heart of the matter.

If you lead a life of truth, then that is what will be exposed to you. Know as a parent we extend our arms to our children and carry them along this journey. Together we can look at life in a different perspective. Some issues we encounter will be challenging, but faced together they will not budge the foundation we have set for ourselves and our family.

Being a parent teaches us to parent the universe and one another. It teaches us to look at the world through a different set of eyes. It teaches us how to care. Maybe before we had children, we cared only for those around us or for ourselves. Now we begin caring about the trails we ourselves leave behind for our children to follow, and for the world as a whole. We begin thinking about our actions and the affect our actions have on our children.

Our children give us the courage to explore a new tomorrow. They give us the strength to fight for what we believe to be in their best interest, and as a result our own best interest. As we care more for our children, we then begin to care that much more for ourselves. Granted our outside appearances may not always reflect that care as we continue down the road of parenting, but the inside flourishes.

It is our duty to also balance our inside and to push the abundance we feel to the outside. Parenting is not about forgetting who we are. It is about sharing who we are with our children. That is not always and easy task to achieve however it is a very necessary one.

Don't stop dreaming just because you have become a parent. Instead, dream even more. Pursue even more of what you want out of life as you are not just striving to achieve these goals for yourself, but for the benefits of your family as a whole.

Exercise 9 – Journal Entry

1. What aspirations did you have before becoming a parent? Have your goals and desires changed?

2. Do you still pursue your dreams or have you placed them off to the side?

3. What realistic goals can you start achieving daily? Weekly? What long term goals do you have? What are you doing to work toward achieving those goals?

Exercise 10

Nurturing PERSONALITIES

One of the many joys of parenting are that we are able to watch our children grow and develop. We are active participants in their lives, but as our children grow our participation fluctuates with being a spectator. There will be times when we have to sit back and watch and allow our children to make choices for themselves.

When our children are little and go towards something that may potentially harm them, we pick them up and tell them they shouldn't do that. We "tell" them about the consequences instead of them having to experience the consequences themselves.

We set boundaries that they can live by, or use to base their own judgments on. These boundaries are foundations that give our children the tools they need to make positive decisions for themselves. That's why when these tools are not present from the parents or guardian, a child can be led down the wrong path, thinking wrong is right and right is wrong.

Children coming from alcoholic or drug addicted parents learn to think that abusive lifestyles are the "correct" way of living. If they are fortunate, they will see how other families live to know the difference between healthy and unhealthy homes. It is then that they learn to question their own environment and pursue other venues, or concepts to which they build their foundation.

If a child is only surrounded by negative behaviors and influences then they will become molded by their environment, which leaves an impression on how they choose to view life, and how they choose to make decisions.

As parents the environment we supply and choose to bring our children up in is crucial. You have to look at yourself as a parent and ask yourself, "Am I living a life that I hope my children would lead?," "Am

I being honest with myself and the world around me?," "Am I being the best that I can be in the life situation I'm currently in?," "Am I making positive life choices?"

If you answer "no" to any of these questions than perhaps you need to adjust your life and strive to make better decisions yourself. You are the mold by which your child will be influenced by. If you have cracks in your shell then your child is also likely to inherit these attributes as well.

When we view how important our role is with raising our children, it puts our faults in a different perspective. Our faults do not go unnoticed by children. In fact once they become vocal enough to communicate and speak to you, they will even be as kind to help point out some of your flaws. This can be quite a comical learning experience for us as parents.

We also begin to see our own behaviors more closely when our little one begins to imitate us. Maybe we respond to certain situations in certain ways, and our child picks up on that. You will be amazed at how your child learns to communicate with each role model in their own particular way. Sit back and observe your little one at work. They are certainly smarter than we sometimes realize them to be.

They know exactly what buttons to push and when to push them. They know how to get what it is they want and their approach varies with each person. What amazing skill children have if we think about it. They have the ability to read a person and know just what to say or do to get the appropriate outcome they are seeking.

Watch your child communicate with their grandparents and then watch how they communicate with you. Watch how they communicate with women verses how they communicate with men. By doing so we are able to see where their strengths and weaknesses are, and we can adjust how we communicate with them.

As children get older they begin to develop their own opinions. They have opinions very early on after birth, they just learn how to express them, and exercise them more, once they begin speech. They can tell you why they do certain things when you ask. They can tell you what they want and what they don't want.

As parents we are able to give our children certain guidelines. However, we cannot overly exert our ideas and concepts to the point that we exclude their freedom. Children have the right to practice their decision making skills daily. They may want the blue toy while you may want them to have the red toy.

Allowing them to exhibit their abilities allows them to feel a great sense of accomplishment when they do make good decisions. We don't realize that all day children are making decisions. They decide what food they want to eat, what they want to wear, what games they feel like playing, and how they want to behave.

Sometimes they make poor decisions and need to be corrected. This is where we as parents come in to explain what they did wrong, and then explain an alternate way of behaving, that would have yielded a positive result. Children are able to understand the laws of cause and effect very early. For example, when they reach for an electric outlet, we are quick to say, "no, no, that's dangerous, or that's bad." They recognize your tone of voice and the actions you make when they are doing something they shouldn't be doing.

When a child is doing something positive it is important to recognize this action and praise them appropriately. This type of response on your part will encourage them to succeed and make them want to perform in a positive manner.

When a child is misbehaving it is also important to let them know that they are acting inappropriately. These types of guidelines define how a child will learn to act later on in life. Either they will learn to put effort into achieving or they will learn to put effort into misbehaving.

Unfortunately there is no perfect way of parenting. You could have someone do everything as "perfect" as they think possible and a child grow up to make bad choices. That is one of the bitter sweet realities of parenting. At some point our children grow up and become adults, and at some point we have to allow them to be adults.

It does not mean that we love them any less. It simply means that we love them enough to let them live life the way they feel is necessary. Yes, there will be pitfalls along the way. There will be challenges that they have to face. There will be important decisions that they will have to make.

Sometimes they may ask for our input and sometimes they will not. Regardless, know that the foundation by which they base these decisions will be the foundation that you set out to establish as a parent.

As a parent our primary goals are to create a safe and loving environment for our children to learn who they are. We nurture their strengths and talents so that their personalities can come out. We give them the security to explore their gifts and discover what it is that they were intended to manifest in the world.

Some of us will raise doctors and lawyers. Some of us will raise military personnel. Some of will raise managers, store clerks, and service people, but know that what we also potentially raise, are future mothers and fathers that will base their influence as parents, on what you provided them with.

May they take home truth and the ability to do right.

Exercise 10 – Journal Entry

1. What steps do you take to nurture your child's unique personality?

2. What goals are you pursuing of your own in addition to your parenting your children?

3. What have your children taken interest in with your lifestyle or talent? What characteristics do they like to imitate?

4. Where would you like to see your family in the future? What long term goals do you have? For yourself? For your partnership? For your children?

www.ingramcontent.com/pod-product-compliance
Lightning Source LLC
Chambersburg PA
CBHW031643170426
43195CB00035B/461